CREATING HARMONIOUS RELATIONSHIPS

CREATING HARMONIOUS RELATIONSHIPS

❧

A Practical Guide to the
Power of True Empathy

REVISED EDITION

ANDREW LECOMPTE

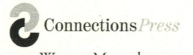

Connections *Press*

Weston, Massachusetts

Published by Connections Press, P. O. Box 443, Weston, MA 02493

The author gratefully acknowledges permission to reprint the following:

Appreciation story. Copyright 1992 by Jo Ann Larsen. Reprinted by permission of Jo Ann Larsen. All rights reserved.

Excerpt from *On Becoming A Person*. Copyright 1961 by Carl Rogers. Reprinted by permission of Houghton Mifflin Company. All rights reserved.

Adaptation of "A Soft Answer" from *Safe and Alive*. Copyright 1981 by Terry Dobson. Printed by permission of The Putnam Publishing Group. All rights reserved.

Prisoner story. Copyright 1992 by Marshall B. Rosenberg. Printed by permission of Marshall B. Rosenberg. All rights reserved.

Excerpt from *To See Differently*. Copyright 1990 by Susan S. Trout. Reprinted by permission of Three Roses Press. All rights reserved.

Excerpts from *How Can I Help? Stories and Reflections on Service*. Copyright 1985 by Ram Dass and Paul Gorman. Reprinted by permission of Alfred A. Knopf, Inc. All rights reserved.

Excerpts from *What We May Be*. Copyright 1982 by Piero Ferrucci. Reprinted by permission of the Putnam Publishing Group. All rights reserved.

Excerpt from John A. Bargh. Lead article in *The Automaticity of Everyday Life, Advances in Social Cognition*, Volume X, 1997, Robert S. Wyer, Ed., by permission of Erlbaum Associates. All rights reserved.

Text Design: Sara Capello

Cover Design: Adam Hay

LCCN: 2023912876

ISBN: 979-8-9887483-0-4

PCN: 9798988748304

Printed in the United States of America

To the memory of my father

Dr. Philip M. LeCompte
1907 – 1998

who wrote in a letter opened by my mother after his death
"I was often difficult to live with, I know,
but not smart enough to know what to do about it."

Introduction to the Revised Edition

I am issuing a Revised Edition of *Creating Harmonious Relationships: A Practical Guide to the Power of True Empathy* in response to popular demand. Individuals and couples want better, closer relationships, but don't know how to achieve them. Yet the simple desire to improve the relationship, coupled with the proven skills in this book, is sufficient to transform the relationship. And the other person doesn't have to cooperate! If you approach the other party with these skills, you will bring about a positive transformation.

This book has helped thousands of people to communicate more effectively and more lovingly. In this book you will learn about "true empathy" – the key to understanding and communicating with people. With it, you will experience the joy and contentment of harmonious relationships.

And, these skills are just as effective in a work environment, allowing you to cut through all sorts of defensiveness and come to agreement.

– Andrew LeCompte

Contents

Acknowledgments

I am deeply indebted to Marshall B. Rosenberg, Ph.D., for developing and teaching the "Nonviolent Communication" model. I am also grateful to all of the participants in my workshops and classes who, through sharing their feelings, hopes and experiences, have helped me refine the communication process presented in this book. The names of people in personal stories have been changed to honor their privacy. I would especially like to thank fellow trainers and friends Carole Starr, Diana McCain, Linda Andrews, Lori Rand, Penny Vernet, Tom Hansen, and Carol Hochstedler for their contributions.

In the field of social psychology I would like to honor the pioneering research of John A. Bargh, Ph.D., of New York University.

I am grateful to Cary Kmet, Martin Koski, and Carol Zickell who introduced me to a spiritual life. Thanks also to Gerald Jampolsky, M.D., Robert Gass, Ph.D., and Brent Haskell, D.O. for further enlightening and clarifying my path.

The assistance of Kelley Conway, my insightful writing coach, and Patricia van der Leun, a remarkable literary agent, was invaluable in bringing this book to fruition.

I have chosen to write in the first person plural as a stylistic standard because it acknowledges our common humanity as we overcome old mental habits to improve our relationships.

Introduction

Difficulties in Relationships

Think of a relationship or a conflict you had with someone that ended unhappily. What bothered you the most about it? Remember what the other person did. What were you thinking and how were you feeling? If you're like most of us, you've agonized about these painful relationships and wondered what went wrong. You've blamed the other person, and in your secret heart you've blamed yourself.

Still, you're a compassionate person, and, even though your feelings were hurt and you said things you regretted, deep down you really cared about the other person and wish things had gone better. If you could rewind the great videotape of life and repair the damage, you would.

Now, you are determined not to repeat the same mistakes. You work hard to keep your relationships healthy and fulfilling, struggling with issues as they appear in your daily life. Here are some of the situations you might be encountering:

- Each time you and your spouse have to make a decision involving conflicting needs, you feel like you get the short end of the stick. When you both are upset and need support, when there's a choice of where to go together for a long weekend, or who needs a new car, you feel that your contributions are not acknowledged and that you're getting less. As a result you begin to feel bad about the relationship and yourself.

- Your boss criticizes something you worked hard on, after you stayed late and used your own personal time. You're left feeling unfairly judged and angry. You worry about your future with this company.

- A friend complains to you continually. When you talk on the phone you find yourself timing her to find out how much time she takes up in the conversation. You like her, but you start resenting the relationship because you feel like you don't matter.

- Every time you decide to make a major change, such as switching your career so you can do the work you love, your parents tell you you'll never succeed, and they advise you to go for the steady pay check instead. You're disappointed not to receive the love and support you'd been hoping for and wish you'd never told them anything.

The question is: *How can you make sure you don't end up with another painful relational conflict or loss?* This is a core issue because we're questioning our essence—whether we are good or bad. We conceive a self-image from how we are in our relationships, and this conception determines every aspect of our lives.

Recognizing the importance of this question in my own life, I embarked on a twenty-year search to find real answers. In the last five years I succeeded, finding and refining a simple but powerful way to understand and empathize with people that went beyond all other methods. The results are contained in this book. Here is my story...

How I Learned to Communicate

I know about ineffective communication from personal experience. My family boasted a doctor father and a mother who was powerful in local politics. Both had lively and critical intellects. Back then, however, we were inept at talking about our feelings, so certain experiences dominated my awareness. My father's outbursts of rage terrified me, and my most vivid early memory is of being paddled with a board in the garage. On the basis of such encounters I determined that I was a bad person. In the isolation of my childhood I didn't know there was another way of relating.

I honed my critical skills, and in high school my talent for pointing out other people's deficiencies earned me the nickname, "the cynic." I remember saying loudly into the hush just after a kid dropped his tray in the cafeteria, "Smooth move, bowels." I felt a glow hearing the laughter around me, but that kid hated me.

I wanted a pretty girlfriend, convinced she would save me from my aching sense of inadequacy. Her love and unfailing support would bring me the security and happiness I craved. I never came close. I was too shy to talk to girls I liked, never mind asking for a date. I soon learned that bourbon took the edge off, and kept my dreams alive in romantic fantasies.

My friendships with men didn't fare much better. I had a good friend, Ray, for a while in college. We got an apartment together, but he started doing unacceptable things, like leaving dirty dishes in the sink. One day I had enough and, not knowing how to confront him, I piled the dishes, greasy frying pan and all, onto his bed. Later I decided he just wasn't good enough and moved out.

With hindsight, I see I wasn't just a poor communicator, I was also unconscious of what was going on inside me. I lived in reaction to other people and used addictive behaviors to mask my inner pain.

I felt closer to my older brother, Tony, than to anyone else in my family. When I was nineteen, Tony died by suicide. My parents came to be with me at the University of Wisconsin in Madison. But, typically for my family, we didn't grieve. That night I shared a hotel room with my father. Lying in bed, I thought about how whenever my brother came to the house the first thing he would say was, "Is Andy home?" I really missed him. Remembering our close connection, I let out a few moaning sobs.

My father said, "Andy, are you alright?"

From lack of experience connecting at a feeling level, I took his question to mean that crying made him uncomfortable and said, "Yeah, I'm OK," and stopped.

Repressing my grief took its toll. I got a severe case of infectious mononucleosis and developed an ulcer, neither of which was diagnosed for months. I lived a thousand miles from home and was convinced I was dying. Then I began to have panic attacks. Waves of terror would surge through me and I'd immediately have to get to a safe place. I told no one about these attacks, fearing I was insane and would be locked in a mental institution. I waited it out for a year and a half, as the attacks slowly lessened.

Although I didn't have friends, I was fortunate to be a good student. I obtained a B.A. in History at the University of Wisconsin and an M.A. at the University of California, winning several fellowships. Happiness in relationships, however, eluded me.

The first positive change to my way of life came in the early 1970s. At the urging of a girlfriend, I began to meditate. Meditation allowed me to become aware of my thoughts. I saw that my mind generated thoughts all by itself and that there was a conscious me who could observe these thoughts. This gave me a new perspective on myself. I realized I had a choice; I could decide which thoughts I wanted to entertain. I didn't need to let myself be controlled by my initial feeling-reactions to other people.

Not long after beginning to meditate, I realized the way I had been living was not bringing me happiness, so I quit my doctoral program in history and began to read psychology. Two authors in particular, Carl Rogers and Viktor Frankl, had a profound influence on me.

In *On Becoming a Person* Carl Rogers describes the healing power of "unconditional positive regard." He validated something most of us know from personal experience, that it feels incredibly good to be listened to and understood by someone who sees only the good in us. His ideas resonated deeply in me. I wanted personal confirmation that I was a good person, and I wanted to experience this in my relationships with others.

I had a negative attitude about life. Viktor Frankl, in *Man's Search for Meaning*, said "the last of the human freedoms [is]– to choose one's attitude in a given set of circumstances, to choose one's own way.... It is this spiritual foundation – that cannot be taken away – that makes life meaningful and purposeful."

I wanted to find that same meaningful conviction. But I knew there was a difference between simply reading Frankl's words about choosing one's attitude and personally integrating that truth. Frankl gained his knowledge the hardest way imaginable: surviving three years in Auschwitz while his father, mother, brother and wife all died at the hands of the Nazis. Frankl explained that there are other ways besides suffering to discover the meaning of life. I was intent on finding meaning in as direct a way as possible.

I entered the most intensive experiential psychology training program I could find. I participated in individual, couples, and group psychotherapy. I taught assertiveness training, transactional analysis, and parent education, earning a second Masters degree in humanistic psychology and organizational development. I then took a series of jobs training executives to manage people effectively.

I became successful and was asked to join the Executive Board of my chapter of the American Society for Training and Development. In the late 1980s I began to consult independently. Although I was highly skilled professionally, my personal life was a series of disasters; my marriage was a good example.

In my psychology program, I fell in love with a woman who was forthright in her humanistic convictions. Yet once I married her, I found I had little ability to articulate my feelings or hopes in personal, intimate situations. I wasn't able to tell her when I felt hurt, sad or afraid. I feared she would see me as weak and would reject me, so I hid those thoughts and feelings. I then projected my inability to communicate onto her and resented her for not being able to guess what I really wanted. After several years I had stored up enough grievances against her to justify to myself that she was an inconsiderate, unloving person. We divorced.

I expected that when she left the trouble in my life would go with her. But as I sat in my silent house, I was shocked to discover that I was only the shell of a person. I lay on the bed with no life energy, unable to work. Then the panic attacks came back. I realized that my life didn't work. I wasn't better than other people; and trying to be "right" in my judgments of them made things worse. My worldview was bankrupt. I hit a terrible bottom of despair, depression, and suicidal thoughts.

By now, however, I had a wonderful young son. Rather than give him up, I began to look harder for answers.

I reentered psychotherapy and found myself unable to cry. I committed myself to learning how. I put together a "crying folder" of pictures of my son and my brother. I wrote a description of the day my son, in the hopes of keeping his parents together, first accepted putting on his Sunday clothes without a fuss. I wrote about how great I felt the day I beat my brother at chess and my exultation when I finally pinned him wrestling. Tony said that I was just getting too strong for him. It was only years later that I recalled he had a genius IQ, was six years older than me and was the undefeated captain of his wrestling team. He had let me win at chess and at wrestling because he loved me.

Looking though this file I could begin to cry; then I would keep myself at it, even talking out loud, telling my son I was sorry, telling my brother I was grateful for all he'd done for me and that I wished I could have been there for him, too. After crying hard I would feel deeply relieved. The panic attacks stopped and never came back.

I also went to support groups and began to develop an inner life. At one of these groups I met Cary, a man with a past as tortured as mine. But he was now happy and serene. I noticed him because when he told his story he cried and was unashamed. I gained the courage to ask him to sponsor me. He became my good friend, the first man with whom I could be completely honest and not made to feel ashamed for feeling weak or afraid. Cary also attended meetings to discuss the book, A Course in Miracles, and invited me to come along.

The course provided me with some important understandings: that I was essentially good, and that my inaccurate perception of other people led me into conflict with them. Forgiving them would lead me to inner peace. By "forgive" the course means to stop judging other people on incomplete evidence and see and accept their goodness instead. The course gave me a better understanding of my mind, pulling together much of what I had already learned. But how to apply this abstract knowledge in face-to-face emotional conflict situations still eluded me.

In 1993, my music teacher handed me a videotaped presentation by Dr. Marshall Rosenberg, founder of the Center for Nonviolent Communication. As I watched Marshall interacting with people I suspected he had what I was looking for. I decided to participate in one of his intensive weekend workshops.

Dr. Rosenberg listened closely, his eyes intent, his body still and open. I was moved by his ability to connect at a feeling level with participants and to facilitate healing of old wounds. He did a role-play with a young woman who wanted to forgive the dying father who had abused her. Marshall helped her to say what she really felt, that in spite of the anger at the trauma she had experienced at his hands, in spite of her sadness at being unable to find happiness with men, she still loved her father. As Marshall role-played her father, I could understand how much he loved his daughter and how horrible he felt about what he had done to her. As her old pain surfaced, was released and replaced by love, everyone in the room was deeply moved. Her healing helped us all.

I saw in Marshall's "nonviolent communication" model a way to connect at the heart that transformed people's attitudes toward each other. It was unconditionally loving. Attacker and defender, victimizer and victim, were gently moved from what at first appeared to be intractable differences to mutual understanding and appreciation. Here were improvements on everything I had learned so far about communication and a way to put into practice what I had studied in *A Course in Miracles*.

The following year I completed Marshall Rosenberg's "Facilitating Nonviolent Communication Training" program in Switzerland. It was a life-changing experience for me. I learned that it wasn't just Marshall Rosenberg who could transform perception and resolve deep conflicts harmoniously. Anyone could grasp and apply these skills. I committed myself to mastering and teaching them.

When I returned to the United States, my personal life changed dramatically for the better. Practicing the skills, I became more conscious, forgiving and happy. I am now in a healthy intimate relationship and engaged to be married. My relationship with my former wife has turned from bitterness to positive cooperation. She recently invited me to her housewarming party. After twenty years of icy silence, I have established a warm connection with my old friend Ray. And my son's teacher told me she had overheard him telling a classmate, "I have a great dad."

I have adapted the "nonviolent communication" model into a conscious communication program, integrated into a broad psychological and spiritual perspective. In 1995 I founded a training organization to teach conscious communication and trained facilitators. As a result many hundreds of people have now experienced the joy and satisfaction of transforming their relationships. Through my ongoing study of social psychology I have found even clearer explanations for why we act as we do, how to be aware of and express what we feel and to hear what other people are hoping for when they may not even realize it.

A New Psychology

This is not just another communication book teaching canned statements and formats that are artificial and don't produce real change. This book goes to the source.

Creating Harmonious Relationships offers a new understanding of how your mind works. You will learn a startling truth—that your unconscious mind is controlling your life. Mistaken unconscious judgments lead you into damaging arguments and fights that are completely unnecessary.

While this is alarming, it is also good news, because you can't change something you are unaware of. This book will show you how to recognize your unconscious judgments so that you can transcend conflict and form positive connections with people.

It is not enough to rephrase unconscious judgments; you must achieve a shift in consciousness. *Creating Harmonious Relationships* will show you, step by step, how to

1. recognize your unconscious judgments as they happen,

2. become conscious with specific centering techniques, and

3. communicate with others so they become conscious.

This book will teach you to connect with the good in other people. This is a different goal than that typically pursued in communication. In typical communication both parties are operating unconsciously, and even with new language the unconscious remains in control.

For example, imagine that your friend Nancy says, "I'm getting sick and tired of Frank always dismissing my ideas as naïve. He ignores them and goes right ahead with his own plan."

Your empathic response to Nancy is, "It sounds like you're angry that Frank never goes along with your ideas." This response is well intended, but it confirms Nancy's unconscious fear that Frank is bad. As Nancy continues to focus on Frank as the problem, he will defend himself. Your empathy has only exacerbated the conflict.

There is a better approach.

A truly empathic response would be, "Nancy, are you frustrated because you'd like your ideas to be appreciated?" This response taps into what Nancy really wants—to be heard and appreciated. It shifts her mind away from the negative judgment of Frank and she becomes more conscious of her positive intention. She realizes that, yes, she really does want to have her ideas heard and appreciated. With this recognition, she can begin to think and communicate about how this could happen.

Connecting with the good intentions in another person is true empathy. In this process the conscious mind of the other person wakes up. This transforms the situation and allows a resolution in which both people win. There is tremendous power in this simple idea.

This book will teach you how to override your unconscious judgments with conscious thought, and then how to listen and speak in a new way that is simple but effective.

What This Book Offers You

Conflicts are daily occurrences and many are mishandled, leading to anger, frustration, and sometimes even physical violence. Unconscious judgments are the cause. Without awareness of how to override your unconscious, you will remain trapped in cycles of attack and defense.

Here is the solution. Using clear language and entertaining examples, *Creating Harmonious Relationships* teaches you how to consciously improve any and all of your relationships. It shows, step by step:

- how to become aware when an unconscious decision is moving you toward conflict,
- how to use conscious override to create a positive connection instead,
- how to listen effectively to find what the other person is really feeling and intending,
- how to manage feelings, particularly anger and guilt,
- how to remain centered by not taking other people's attack language personally,
- how to speak powerfully without judging, coercing, or attacking,
- how to carry out challenging communications, and
- how to resolve conflicts while enhancing relationships at the same time.

Conscious communication encourages people to disclose their feelings and the positive intentions that cause those feelings. Connecting at this deeper level results in profoundly satisfying relationships. This book will show you how to respond consciously, even in the heat of a conflict situation, and how to dramatically improve your connection with all the people in your life.

Let's get started.

What disturbs people's minds is not events but their judgments on events.

– EPICTETUS

CHAPTER ONE

What Goes Wrong?

Think of the last time you had a conflict with someone, an interaction that went badly, one that you stewed about afterwards. Bill, an engineer taking one of my evening classes, told this story about a nonverbal communication. Can you guess how the people felt?

Bill's Story

Last Saturday when he went to have his car's engine adjusted, Bill took his son along. The "couple of minutes" fix ended up taking two hours, and his son got bored. So, to cheer him up, Bill told him they'd buy a toy at the toy store across the street on the way home. But by the time they were ready to go, the traffic was really heavy. They sat in the car waiting for a break to get across the street. Every time there was a gap on their side, the other side was a steady stream of cars. A car behind Bill kept inching up until it was almost touching his bumper.

Finally, a space opened and Bill hit the gas. His car jumped forward, but at that same instant a Ford sedan in the toy store lot backed up and blocked the entrance. Bill braked to avoid hitting it and his car was left suddenly in front of the oncoming traffic. A pickup truck hurtled right at them.

"He's going to hit us!" Bill thought.

The truck screeched to a halt at the last second. A horn blasted. The huge shiny grill bobbed up and down in his son's window.

Finally the car blocking Bill moved out of the way. As Bill pulled off the road, the guy in the pickup truck honked again, really leaning on it. Out of the corner of his eye Bill thought he saw the guy's mouth working. Bill wished he'd been driving a car equipped for James Bond, with a hidden fireball cannon to blow the guy away.

Most of us have had a driving experience like Bill's. As we talked about it in the group, I recorded the feelings Bill had about the incident and why. He felt:

- embarrassed to have made a reckless move in front of his son,
- scared to have endangered their lives, and
- angry at the guy in the truck for honking twice.

We took a look at what might have been going on with the pickup driver. As we talked about it in the group, we concluded that with his second honk, the pickup driver was blaming Bill for acting stupidly and dangerously. The honk made a moral statement that what Bill did wasn't just a simple, easily overlooked mistake. Bill had done something "wrong," which in turn implied he did it from some selfish or evil motive, as if he were so intent on meeting his own needs that he didn't care if he endangered others. The second honk was intended to wake Bill up, to correct and punish him.

"I'm not a bad driver," Bill insisted. "How could I know that car was going to back up at that second? No one had gotten into it. It was just sitting there."

Why did Bill want to defend his actions? Because he never intentionally does things wrong. He's always trying his best, given what he knows in the moment. Isn't that why we each feel upset when someone judges us in a negative way? We may have made a mistake, but we were just trying to do something good, like buy a toy for our child.

Why did Bill feel so angry that he wanted to blast the other driver? Being judged hurts. We view other people who make false, negative judgments of us as wrong and aggressive. Of course, we never do that. We are alert, kind-hearted, and reasonable.

Maggie and Kristen

In another group, when I asked for interactions that people felt badly about, Maggie, a graphic artist, told this story.

She had just bought a new pen to use in her office at home and her thirteen-year-old daughter, Kristen, saw it and tried it out. She showed her mother the distinctive look the pen gave to her handwriting.

The next morning Kristen left to catch the school bus while Mom was still upstairs. A few minutes later when Maggie went to her workspace, she couldn't find the pen. She looked on the desk and under it, then tried all the drawers, growing more frustrated.

Then she remembered how much her daughter liked it. She imagined Kristen wanting to show her friends at school how neat her handwriting looked. She thought of how impressing her peer group seemed to be Kristen's primary goal in life. Maggie imagined her, unable to find a pen for school, casually taking her mother's.

Whatever Kristen's rationale for taking it, Maggie needed that pen to complete an advertisement, and she was angry.

As soon as Kristen came in the door Maggie said, "I am very upset that you took my pen. Where is it?"

"I don't have it, Mom. I didn't take your pen." Later, Maggie found it under some papers on her computer table.

Maggie was embarrassed for having thought badly of her daughter. It had seemed like such a cut-and-dried case. Maggie is not alone in making mistaken judgments. It is easy for us to judge another person's motivation, so easy we hardly notice it.

Two patterns that have consistently emerged as I've worked with people and their conflict situations are:

- people almost always think they know what is motivating another person's behavior and
- they are usually mistaken.

The honker thought Bill wasn't paying proper attention to safe driving and needed to be corrected. Maggie was certain that her daughter had selfishly taken the pen. Like them, we judge the motivation of other people much more frequently than we realize, and our judgments get us into a lot of trouble.

Have you ever been in a relationship with someone you really enjoyed and then were confused and upset when it started to disintegrate? You are intelligent and kind. So is the other person. Or at least they appeared to be before the trouble started.

Jennifer and Paul Fight (their words)

Paul and Jennifer had been married for two years. They loved each other and counted on each other's support. One day, Jen's boss criticized her work. She walked out to her car fuming mad, got in and slammed the door. *I hate that jerk, Steve*, she thought. *I can't wait to get home and tell Paul about this.*

As she drove in she was delighted to see Paul's car in the driveway. She rushed in the door and said: "I am so fed up with Steve. He told me he needed a written statement of our position on environmental protection before his flight. I saw he was anxious, so I got right to work and wrote a piece I thought was really good.

"He looked at it and what does he say? 'This is useless. I can't use this.' Well for crying out loud! I spent two hours on it! He asked for the dumb thing; it seemed a little off the wall, but what's new about that? Anyway, I put all my work aside and did it for him and then all he can say to me is 'This is useless.' What a total jerk!"

"Jen," Paul replied, "if it didn't make a whole lot of sense to you when he first asked for it, why didn't you find out what he really wanted before you did it?"

"What! So it's all my fault! You guys are so smart and I'm the ditsy woman who doesn't have a clue how to figure out what's going on. Let me tell you something. I am not stupid! And I do not need to be criticized by you!"

"Hey, calm down. I'm not criticizing you. If you get this defensive at work, I can see how it could cause you trouble."

"Listen, Mister Cool, when I want your opinion on how inappropriate I am at work, I will ask. Until then, keep it to yourself." She stomped out of the room.

Jennifer wanted to talk with Paul about her painful experience and get some emotional support. Paul wanted to help her. What went wrong? After this argument neither understood why they had been attacked.

This pattern of communication continued, off and on, throughout their marriage. They tried counseling, which helped temporarily. But after they stopped attending sessions, they began to slip back into their old ways of communicating. As they became more and more frustrated, their attacks became more vicious. Finally, they got divorced.

If we are going to do better in our relationships, we need to be able to understand what went wrong with Jen and Paul. To start, let's look at what their thoughts might have been if we slowed the interaction down.

Jennifer and Paul Fight (their thoughts)

Just before they spoke Jen was thinking: *I feel terrible after what happened at work. I really want to connect with Paul.* And Paul was thinking: *Good, Jen's home. I'm happy to see her.*

Then Jen said: "I am so fed up with Steve. All he can say to me is 'This is useless.' What a total jerk!" And she was thinking: *I'm hurt and frustrated. Maybe I made a mistake, but I worked hard for him and even got behind on my own work. At least he could have acknowledged my effort to help him. I want Paul to understand this.*

Paul thought: *Damn that guy! Poor Jen. She wasted all that time and then got put down. What can I say that will be helpful? It sounds like she could avoid this kind of problem in the future if she checked for the details of what was really wanted.*

So he said: "If it didn't make a whole lot of sense to you when he first asked for it, why didn't you find out what he really wanted before you did it?"

Jen thought: *Oh, no! He's blaming it all on me! I can't be understood anywhere. Neither of them sees that I'm generous and caring. They only see me as incompetent. Well I'm not! And the last thing I need when I'm looking for understanding and support is to have Paul tell me I'm the problem.*

She said, "Oh for crying out loud! So it's all my fault! You guys are so smart and I'm the ditsy woman who doesn't have a clue how to figure out what's going on. Let me tell you something. I am not stupid! And I do not need to be criticized by you!"

Paul thought: *I'm just trying to help. I give her my best suggestion and she throws it back in my face! I'm hurt. I didn't say she was stupid. She's turning her anger at Steve onto me and falsely accusing me of criticizing her. That's not fair! I need to calm her down and show her how she's overreacting.*

And he said: "Hey, calm down. I'm not criticizing you. If you get this defensive at work, I can see how that could cause you trouble."

Jennifer thought: *He denies criticizing me! Then, after making me furious, he accuses me of being defensive. He doesn't have a clue how I am at work. I'm not defensive until Paul attacks me. He's certainly not giving me the love and affection I wanted. This is so unfair! I'd better get out of here before I break down in front of this unsympathetic, antagonistic creep.*

"Listen, Mister Cool, when I want your opinion on how inappropriate I am at work, I will ask. Until then, keep it to yourself." And she left the room.

Jen and Paul weren't conscious of their thoughts. The argument happened too fast for them to know what they hoped for in the conversation. Their failure to voice their initial positive thoughts has a lot to do with their lack of awareness of what was really going on inside them. Then they each made significant misinterpretations and negative judgments of each other. But why would two intelligent people do this? Specifically:

1. Why did Paul think the best way to help Jen was to tell her how to prevent the problem?

2. Why did Jen interpret Paul to be blaming her and saying she was incompetent?

3. Why did Paul feel unfairly accused and need to call her "defensive"?

4. Why did Jen blame Paul for making her angry and want to end the relationship?

Their Problem

All these questions have the same answer. Thinking too quickly wasn't their problem. The problem was the kind of thoughts they had. All the thoughts that caused this fight and killed this relationship between two people who loved each other had one thing in common—they were all *negative judgments*.

1. Why did Paul think the best way to help Jen was to tell her how to prevent the problem? Because Paul judged Jen's handling of her boss's request as inadequate.

2. Why did Jen interpret Paul to be blaming her and saying she was incompetent? Because Paul was judging her performance. She focused on that, and she judged that Paul's intent was to criticize her, blame her and pronounce her incompetent.

3. Why did Paul feel unfairly accused and need to call her "defensive"? Because she had judged him to be blaming her. He felt misunderstood. And he then judged that her intention was to blame him, so he called her behavior "defensive," implying such behavior was not a reasonable response to him.

4. Why did Jen blame Paul for making her angry and want to quit the relationship? Because she judged his intent was to attack her, so she attacked back.

Jen and Paul behaved like sharks on a feeding frenzy of negative judgment. Judgment is potent stuff. Let's take a closer look at it.

Judging, in the context of interpersonal communication, is interpreting the goodness or badness of the motive behind a person's action or words. *The judgment implies that the person did what they did on purpose.* Someone's negative judgment of our behavior indicates they think we had a bad intention. And who but a bad person would do something hurtful on purpose? When someone judges our intention as bad, they are judging our worth. Their negative judgment is an attack on our identity.

Negative judgment also includes the interpretation of another person as defective. We saw this in Paul's judgment of how Jen handled her work situation. His determination that her performance could have been improved, without any other qualifying information, could easily be interpreted as implying that Jen performs poorly because she's defective.

Negative judgments conflict with our perceptions of ourselves as "good." Good means "positive or desirable in nature, worthy of respect, competent and kind." I like to think of myself as good. I'm sure you do too. In fact, in my workshops with hundreds of people, many of whom have been incarcerated, I have yet to find a person who didn't think of himself as essentially good.

"Bad" according to the dictionary means "not achieving an adequate standard, evil, sinful." Yet for the same behavior that we might condemn someone else as bad, we would judge ourselves innocent. Because we know what we intend: *We just made a mistake.*

When we make a mistake, we know we started with good motives, but something we hadn't foreseen occurred and someone got hurt. If we had known that someone was going to get hurt, we wouldn't have done what we did.

Other people's intentions, however, are invisible, so we often perceive them as bad. As a result, our negative judgment violates their self-concept as whole, non-defective people. Who but an evil person would have an evil intention? Understanding that someone has made a mistake versus judging them as morally wrong makes a world of difference. This is why judgment matters so deeply to people. When they see their self-image threatened, they need to do something about it, and quickly.

Simply putting ourselves in the role of judge carries a risk. A judge is "one who makes estimates as to worth, quality or fitness." But if we are equal, just who does a person think he is to be my judge? His assuming a right to judge me implies that he considers himself better than me and that he thinks he knows what is going on inside me. But my thoughts are not visible. I know them; others don't.

This discussion of judgment is easy to understand. So why then did Paul and Jen fall into judging each other? What can psychology tell us?

Let's look at the psychology of perception and response. Most people, and many psychologists, would say it works like this:

1. A social event occurs.

2. We see and hear what is going on.

3. We make a conscious evaluation of the people and their actions.

4. We consider an appropriate response.

5. We respond.

Usually we are accurate in our perception, fair in our evaluation and appropriate in our response. But sometimes we make a mistake in perception; sometimes we make a poor evaluation, and sometimes we make an inappropriate response. We learn from these experiences. We try to be more perceptive, more understanding, and more knowledgeable. The more we practice, the better we get.

There is one sticky problem, however. From time to time we see people behave irrationally. They misunderstand us, even hate us, and verbally attack us in a way that makes us confused. Their behavior cannot be rationally explained. The great scientific psychologist Sigmund Freud studied the effects of the unconscious on the personality. Freudian psychology describes the irrational basis of human behavior and the hidden emotional content of our everyday actions.

A Quick Review

Freud described the personality as three dynamic systems: the *id*, the *ego*, and the *superego*. The id is present at birth and is the source of our unconscious impulses to fulfill our instincts and needs. Reacting immediately to sensory stimuli, it tries to get rid of pain and tension and to find pleasure. The id is infantile, irrational, and selfish. We can only know about it from its symptoms, as when a child impulsively hits someone. It cannot learn or be modified by experience. Clearly, the id's reflexes are too primitive to bring us satisfaction in the world.

The *ego* system of the personality develops later and deals with the world. The ego realizes that gratification must sometimes wait in order to happen in realistic and appropriate ways, so it attempts to balance and control the id. Learning through the process of socialization, the ego can think and problem-solve. It uses the senses to rapidly scan the environment and select only what is relevant to the current problem. As it learns, it becomes more efficient.

The *superego* is the moral conscience of the personality and it determines right from wrong. It also attempts to keep the id in check. The superego represents the child's assimilation of his parents' moral authority concerning what is good and bad, which allows the child to maintain the parents' approval and avoid their disapproval. The superego is the representation of both his parents' and his culture's traditional values.

As the ego and superego attempt to restrain the id, the three systems dynamically exchange psychic energy. By explaining this dynamic, Freud provided an explanation for irrational behavior. People experience inner tension because their id wants to do something impulsive and their superego says, "No that's bad." So their ego comes to the rescue with irrational, unconscious defense mechanisms to help them cope. One of these defense mechanisms is projection.

Projection works like this. Jack has a problem with Bob. Jack's id decides, "I hate Bob and want to hurt him." But Jack's superego says that hating and hurting are bad and not acceptable. Jack is experiencing inner deadlock and tension. So Jack's ego resolves this deadlock by *reversing who is doing the bad thing.* He now says, "Bob hates *me* and wants to hurt *me*." He has projected his own id's hate and aggression onto Bob.

So Bob is now the bad guy and Jack can hate and hurt him. Jack's three systems are all happy doing this. Jack's superego thinks self-defense is good and honorable; Jack's id is getting to hate and hurt Bob; and Jack's ego has resolved the mind's inner tension by projecting the evil motive outside onto Bob. Because his projection is entirely unconscious, Jack proceeds to hate and hurt Bob without a qualm.

While it works for Jack, we clearly see that his projection is irrational. But if we examine our own behavior we would doubtless say that we don't indulge in projection. That is because projection is always unconscious so we *don't have a clue* when we do it.

We do notice, however, that other people, like Jack, may hate us and try to hurt us from time to time. We assume that these other people, lacking our mental and emotional resources, use projection against us. It is very uncomfortable to think that our own unconscious has a powerful and unpredictable influence on us.

Maybe you don't want to believe this—I certainly didn't. But one night I learned how wrong I could be. Here is the story:

My Projection

During my divorce, I lived in a bundle of fearful thoughts. I was desperate enough to seek help, but the first time I went to a support group for people from alcoholic families I also wanted to maintain my "I'm OK" façade. I felt extremely nervous as I entered the building. I was thinking, *Will these people check me out and think I'm mentally ill or pathetically incompetent? Will I be looked down on, shamed, humiliated?*

During the meeting the people talked about having difficulties relating with other people, but no one pried into anybody else's personal affairs. I liked the basic meeting format and even identified with the feelings and situations of several of the people who spoke. Gradually, I became less fearful. A few people smiled and said goodnight to me, and, as I drove home, I decided to try it again the following week.

The next week in walked a guy wearing baggy pink shorts and a clashing Hawaiian shirt. He had a punk haircut with a little rat's tail down the back of his neck. His gum-chewing face was pitted with large acne sores. Laughing loudly, he high-fived two of the men and greeted several other people.

Oh, brother, I thought, *if they let jerks like him in the group, this is not for me.* The only reason I didn't leave was that I thought the orderly format of the meeting would keep him from being the center of attention. But the meeting wasn't starting. It appeared no one had signed up to chair. To my horror, "Pink Shorts" picked up the meeting agenda and said "If nobody else wants to, I'll lead."

Oh no! Please, somebody help! I thought. *Don't let this moron chair.* No one spoke up. *What a bunch of losers,* I thought. *Now I've wasted most of my evening, but at least I can leave at the break.*

Part of chairing the meeting involved telling your story; so Pink Shorts, who's name turned out to be John, started telling his. He told how his father was an alcoholic. Often when his dad didn't come home, his mother would get really worried and send him out onto the streets of Philadelphia to find his father. Usually John found him in a bar or stumbling around outside. Sometimes his dad was so drunk he couldn't walk. John helped him get back home, often with schoolmates and neighbors looking on.

His dad wasn't responsible with money either. Once he was viciously beaten by loan sharks right in front of John. John felt sorry for his mother, who worked all day in a department store, because he knew curvature of the spine made prolonged standing painful for her.

One day his father, then in his early thirties, died on the kitchen floor from drinking. His mother was weeping. John put his arm around her shaking shoulders and told her, at age eight, not to worry, that he would get a job and make everything all right for her.

"My mom had suffered incredibly, year after year, and I wanted so much for her to be happy," he said.

John tried to keep talking but tears filled his eyes. He swallowed once, then a few more times. My eyes started to burn. Here was a man of enormous compassion, speaking the truth from his heart.

I was to learn that he always did that. He became my best friend. He loved himself and was able to love other people, and, more profoundly than any other human being, he taught me that I too was worthy of being loved. That was the greatest gift of my life.

And I almost missed it. My judgment of Pink Shorts was way off.

I had walked into the meeting in a fearful state, concerned with how I would impress the group. My id was obsessed with wanting to look better than other people. I then unconsciously projected my obsession with making a good impression onto John. I decided that the reason he wore loud clothes was to call attention to himself and so I judged him as self-centered. His exuberant greeting of other people I judged as boastful swagger.

I totally missed the warm caring and joy that John was demonstrating. Why? Because I was so frightened I couldn't see the truth about him. If I'd left before learning more of what was going on inside him, I would have missed a generous heart that lifted me out of my self-centered depression and into a new life.

Why did I project onto John? Perhaps because his hairstyle, bright clothing, and chewing gum were at odds with my conservative New England background. Shouldn't I have known better? I always tried to be open-minded and fair. I'd been trained in humanistic psychology. Why couldn't I give John the benefit of the doubt?

Psychologists have been researching this very problem. Their startling answer is that I couldn't help projecting on him and judging him negatively.

Everything one encounters is preconsciously screened and
classified as either good or bad, within a fraction of a second
of encountering it.

– DR. JOHN BARGH

CHAPTER TWO

What Makes Us Go Wrong?

What Psychologists Have Known about Unconscious Processes

Psychologists have been aware that the mind makes some decisions automatically, without conscious attention. We can drive, for example, without giving it a thought. This wasn't true when we were first learning. Then, not popping the clutch took our full attention. But as adults, most of us drive unconsciously. We cruise down familiar streets while talking to a passenger, listening to the radio, or planning the future.

Because of the tremendous amount of data streaming in to the mind every second from our senses, our mind's ability to perform routine tasks unconsciously is essential. The human eye, for example, scans two billion bits of data per second. If all this data were not already organized somehow, the conscious mind would have to start from scratch to figure out what each pattern of light and dark meant. We simply can't afford to consciously process all the data every time we move our eyes. It would take all day just to get dressed. So the mind uses automatic processes to organize data and carry out routine tasks. Unconscious processing is much faster than conscious processing.

An automatic process is similar to multitasking on a computer. The computer can be downloading a program from the Internet (the routine task) while the operator is using the computer for word-processing (the conscious task).

Here is an example of how an automatic process develops:

When a child is young, her parents show her a chair and say the word, "chair." Gradually the child learns that a certain pattern of visual data mean a chair. As the child looks for similar patterns, she is able to recognize other chairs more quickly. Eventually, her mind delegates chair-finding entirely to an unconscious process and conscious thought is no longer required.

While psychologists have known about automatic processes for a long time, they assumed our minds consciously monitored them to make sure they were doing what we wanted.

If unconscious processes are the cause of the irrational behavior that destroys our relationships, we need to know the answers to the following questions:

1. What triggers unconscious processes?
2. What do unconscious processes do?
3. How much of the time are we acting unconsciously?
4. Can we control or influence the unconscious so we can be more accurate in our judgments, more able to understand and get along with other people?

The Breakthrough Discoveries

On August 8, 1995, Daniel Goleman reported some startling psychological research results on the front page of the *New York Times* science section. Dr. John Bargh and Dr. Shelly Chaiken, both at New York University, measured the existence of the unconscious judgment process. The following account is condensed from the great number of experiments they performed to show the heart of their breakthrough.

The researchers used two simple psychological tools to measure the judgment process. The first tool was a list of words. There are some words that everybody likes and judges as good, such as "friend" and "beautiful." There are others that everybody dislikes and judges as bad, such as "cancer" and "death." And there are many words in the middle that some people associate with good and others with bad. Prior to the experiment, the scientists had each person who was a subject of the experiment rate words until each had a list of words which they had judged good and a list they judged bad.

The other tool was a tachistoscope. A tachistoscope flashes a brief, timed image on a screen for durations as brief as a quarter of a second. Remarkably, at that speed the subject's conscious mind does not know anything happened. They don't think they saw anything. *But their unconscious mind sees the image.* If the flashed image is a word, the unconscious mind reads, understands and reacts to the word, even though the subject's conscious mind doesn't know that there was anything to see. In this way the tachistoscope provides direct access to the unconscious mind.

In the experiment the scientists presented the subjects with two words, one right after the other. The first word was flashed on the screen at a quarter second, too fast to be consciously visible. The second, or "target" word, was projected on the screen long enough to be visible. The subjects were asked to press one button if they thought the target word was "good" or another button if they thought it was "bad."

Here is an example. Imagine Jill is the subject. She is sitting and looking at a blank screen, ready to see a word and push either the "good" button or the "bad" button. Unbeknownst to Jill, the scientists flash the word "friend," which carries a good judgment for her, on the screen for a quarter of a second. She's doesn't know she saw it. Then they put the target word "beautiful" on the screen; Jill quickly judges it as "good" and pushes the "good" button.

The scientists found that all the subjects, like Jill, also responded quickly if they judged both words as good. They also responded quickly if they judged both words as bad, as in a pairing of the flashed word "disease" and the visible target word "nasty."

But watch what happens to Jill when the flashed word has a different judgment than the target word.

This time the scientists flash the word "cancer" on the screen for a quarter of a second. Jill is not aware that anything happened and, as before, the target word "beautiful" appears. Jill judges beautiful as "good" and pushes the "good" button, but this time it takes her more time than in the last example.

In both examples, Jill saw and judged the target word "beautiful" and hit the "good" button. In the first example she saw "beautiful" and was *quick* to judge it good. In the second example she saw "beautiful: and was *slow* to judge it good.

The only explanation for the slower time is that her unconscious mind had first judged the flashed word "cancer." Then, when she saw "beautiful," she had to reverse her judgment from bad to good and *this reversal of judgment took extra time.*

This time difference held true for everyone. Each time the target word required a judgment different from the flashed word, responses were slower. The subjects needed extra time to switch their minds from their judgment of the flashed word to a different judgment of the target word.

The experiment proved that their minds had seen and judged the flashed word, unconsciously, within a quarter of a second.

Bargh and Chaiken performed many experiments similar to this one using other images such as pictures of people's faces. In all cases, when the flashed image was negative and the visible image was positive, the subjects took longer to respond. This indicated they were making instantaneous, unconscious judgments.

The scientists thought of what factors might provide alternate explanations for the results and performed additional experiments to screen those factors out. They consistently found the same pattern of instantaneous, preconscious judgment taking place. Bargh concluded: "Therefore, everything one encounters is preconsciously screened and classified as either good or bad, within a fraction of a second after encountering it."

This experiment demonstrates that our unconscious mind always judges everything it perceives, and it does so within a *fraction* of a second. No word, sound or face is neutral. We interpret everything in the world as good or bad, before our conscious mind even knows what it is.

As a result of these experiments, we know a great deal more about the unconscious. The various experiments have provided answers to the first two of our questions from the beginning of the chapter:

1. What triggers unconscious processes?

    Everything we see, hear, touch, taste or smell is interpreted and acted upon by the automatic processes of the unconscious mind. This includes social events and the actions of others.

2. What do the unconscious processes do?

    Unconscious mental processes make three very important kinds of decision: perceptual, evaluative and motivational. The unconscious mind makes all of these decisions simultaneously within a fraction of a second. See Table 1.

Let's look at these different automatic, unconscious decisions briefly one at a time.

Table 1 – **What Our Unconscious Does**

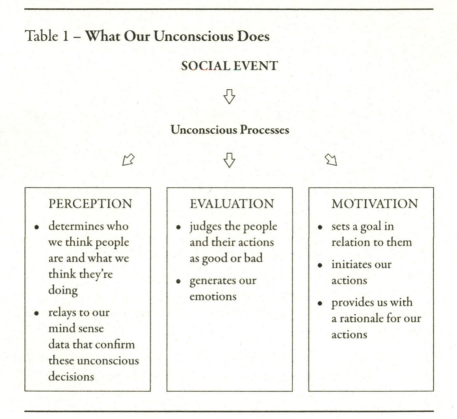

SOCIAL EVENT

⇩

Unconscious Processes

PERCEPTION	EVALUATION	MOTIVATION
• determines who we think people are and what we think they're doing	• judges the people and their actions as good or bad	• sets a goal in relation to them
• relays to our mind sense data that confirm these unconscious decisions	• generates our emotions	• initiates our actions
		• provides us with a rationale for our actions

Perception: The unconscious determines our perceptions—our recognition and interpretation of sensory stimuli. It decides what the light waves and sound waves in the environment mean. The unconscious makes sense out of what we see and hear. Because of the overwhelming amount of sense data present, the unconscious is very selective. It selects and passes on to our conscious awareness only those sight and sound impressions of a particular event that confirm its *initial judgment*. In this way *the unconscious determines everything we see and hear*. We think we see and hear an objective reality, but we do not.

Evaluation: The unconscious evaluates everything and everybody as positive or negative and this judgment determines our feelings. If the unconscious judges someone as good, we will have positive feelings, such as joy, and be drawn toward them. On the other hand, if the unconscious judges a person or their behavior as bad, we will see them as a threat and feel afraid, angry or sad, depending on the specific circumstances. This is the source of our irrational negative judgments.

Motivation: The unconscious determines our motivation relative to what we perceive. Derived from the Latin verb motere, "to move," motivation refers to the desire that causes us to move toward a goal. For example, we may be stimulated by the smell of breakfast cooking and our hunger motivates us to seek the goal, food. This stimulus-motivation-goal process gets us out of bed and into the kitchen. Our motivation is linked to the goal.

Unconscious Influences

In 1992 Senator Bob Packwood was accused of sexual harassment. He denied it, but after a lengthy investigation the Senate Ethics Committee recommended that he be expelled from the Senate and he resigned. Yet the senator's diaries clearly reveal that he did not understand that his behavior was harassment. His lack of awareness can be explained by understanding how our mind selects and uses goals.

When we have a goal our unconscious mind influences our behavior in numerous ways to help bring about the goal. For example, when our goal is to achieve something, we automatically concentrate better and become more aware of things that will help us to attain it. Because our goal-states powerfully influence our behavior it is important to know how we set our goals.

Dr. Bargh performed an experiment that radically alters how psychologists have understood the goal setting process.

Using subliminal techniques so that participants were unaware of being primed either way, Bargh primed some participants with achievement-related stimuli and some with neutral stimuli. Then each was given a rack of Scrabble® letters and asked to make as many words as they could in three minutes. When the "stop" signal was given, more than half of the achievement-primed participants continued working, whereas less than a quarter of the neutral-primed participants continued. The obvious conclusion is that *our goals can be set in motion unconsciously*. This process affects our daily lives.

A certain situation can become linked in one's mind with a certain goal state. When we find ourselves in that situation the mind automatically adopts the linked goal. For some men, perhaps including former Senator Packwood, the situation of having power is unconsciously linked to a sexual goal. People in subordinate positions, on the other hand, in his case, women, have a goal of keeping their jobs, and part of that includes being pleasant and smiling.

In this situation the man and the woman are likely to interpret the same behavior differently. She smiles as a professional courtesy. The man interprets her smile as flirtation and makes an advance. She is aware of the power he wields over her job and the implied threat if she doesn't go along. He is not aware of how power influences his perception and does not understand his subsequent behavior as harassment.

In another experiment, Bargh demonstrated that a person likely to be sexually aggressive will find a woman more attractive when his concept of power has been unconsciously primed.

Our goals are particularly important because they determine what we see, think and do. That our goals themselves are often triggered by the unconscious is cause for major concern. Our goals determine our behavior. Once activated, our goals operate on any relevant input without conscious intent or guidance and direct our information-processing and social behavior.

Unconscious goal setting can have serious consequences in social situations, causing us to behave in a way opposite to how we would otherwise behave. Bargh describes an amazing experiment in which participants initially preferred a person displaying polite behavior. But after they were unconsciously triggered for aggressive goals by the experimenters, they reversed themselves and preferred a person displaying aggressive behavior. They didn't have any idea they had been easily manipulated. Bargh concludes, "Judgments are made as a result [of an unconscious goal] which are clearly counter to what the individual would make if he or she intended to process that source of information."

Another study by Bargh found that subjects who were unconsciously influenced with rude words (interrupt, disturb) as part of a language test were four times more likely to behave rudely themselves than were subjects unconsciously influenced with polite words (patient, respectful). Influencing participants' unconscious minds with a behavioral trait such as polite or rude makes the participants more likely to behave that way.

All of the decisions made by the unconscious in response to a social event happen in the same instant and are inextricably bound to each other. We are drawn to approach what we judge to be good and to withdraw from or to push away what we evaluate as bad, and our goals are tied in with our judgments.

Because we are unconscious of these decisions, we don't know what influenced us to act as we did. We think we know why, but our explanations are inaccurate. Actually, our "logical explanations" are after-the-fact rationalizations. *The unconscious always provides a rationalization for our behavior.*

For example, Dr. Bargh cites a study in which a woman, while hypnotized, was told "When you awake you will crawl on your hands and knees." When she woke from hypnosis she began to crawl on her hands and knees. She spontaneously said, "I think I lost an earring down here." In a similar way, our unconscious always gives us plausible explanations for our behavior.

The new understanding of the psychology of perception and response

1. A social event occurs.

2. An automatic set of unconscious mental processes simultaneously:

   - decides what all the involved things, people and actions are, determines their attributes (e.g. "polite," "rude"), and selects sensory information to send to the conscious mind,

   - judges whether they are good or bad and generates our emotions,

   - sets our goal for interacting with them, initiates our actions with them, and even provides us with a "rational" reason for our actions.

Dr. Bargh also answers our third question from the beginning of the chapter: *How much of the time are we acting unconsciously?*

Bargh states that over ninety-nine percent of our "everyday life—thinking, feeling, and doing—is automatic..." or unconscious. "I believe if one is scrupulously honest about the number of times per day that one actually takes more than a half-second to make a decision (one signature of a control or nonautomatic process), the number could be counted on one's fingers... This is a very small percentage of all the perceptions, behaviors, judgments, evaluations and intentions one constantly makes each day. When it does happen—when we do override the automatic process—these occasions are memorable and salient precisely because they are effortful and unusual. As a consequence, we are misled by the greater availability of these occasions in memory into hugely overestimating how often we really do engage in acts of deliberate control."

Unconscious processes combine to create an immediate psychological situation—everything that we know about the world and the individual people in it: what we see and hear, whom we like and dislike, our feelings about them, and our intentions for or against them. The alarming truth is that we are seldom conscious.

Influences beyond our awareness, and therefore beyond our control, are running our lives. This is true virtually all the time. *Our relationships with others, our happiness, and our success in life all hinge on our willingness to become aware that we are subject to unconscious, and therefore irrational, decision-making.* Without this awareness we cannot stop the damaging cycles of misperception, judgment, and attack that crop up in our relationships. What we don't know hurts us and hurts other people.

Humanly we have been taught to judge, criticize, and condemn anybody, any time, anywhere for anything that does not fit our own sense of what is right or wrong..

– *JOEL S. GOLDSMITH*

CHAPTER THREE

The Judge

Dr. Bargh's psychological research has proven that our daily lives are almost entirely under the control of our unconscious. We don't know why we respond as we do to what we're seeing, thinking or doing. The magnitude of this threatens our self-image as intelligent, sentient beings. It certainly explains why we have trouble with the complexities of relationships. And relationships are where the most damaging effects of our lack of conscious awareness occur.

Meet Your Judge

In the first instant of every social event our unconscious mind's primary task is to judge other people as good or bad. For the sake of brevity we will refer to the set of unconscious, automatic processes simply as "the judge."

Our judge's initial determination of a person as good or bad sets our goal for the interaction. If his judgment of a person is good, he sets the goal to connect. If he judges a person as bad, he sets the goal to defend. The defend goal includes the strategies of withdrawal, attack, and changing the other person. The connect goal includes getting closer to the other person, supporting them and accepting them. See Table 2.

Table 2 – Your Judge's Primary Social Task

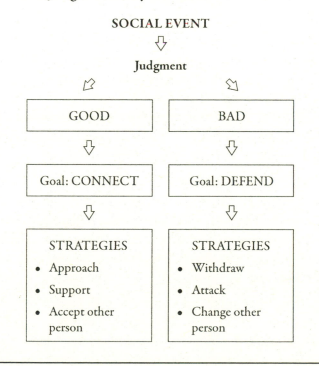

SOCIAL EVENT

⇩

Judgment

GOOD	BAD
Goal: CONNECT	Goal: DEFEND
STRATEGIES • Approach • Support • Accept other person	STRATEGIES • Withdraw • Attack • Change other person

---

Paul's Judge

When Jen came home from work, starting at the moment she walked in the door and reported that her boss had rejected her write-up on environmental protection, Paul's judge was judging "bad." Paul's judge identified with Jen. He thought: *How embarrassing! I hate to make mistakes. I feel inner tension. I need to fix Jen.* Paul's judge chose the defend goal and the strategy of changing Jen. He then thought, *How do I avoid mistakes? By being careful and knowing exactly what is expected. I'll teach this to Jen and fix her. Fixing her will relieve my inner tension.* So Paul suggested to Jen that she should have found out what her boss expected before doing the work.

Jen's judge heard Paul's advice as criticism and chose to defend. Jen said, "So it's all *my* fault! You guys are so smart and I'm the ditsy woman who doesn't have a clue how to figure out what's going on. Let me tell you something; I am not stupid! And I do not need to be criticized you!"

Paul's judge saw this statement of Jen's also as *bad* and maintained his defend goal. His judge used this sense data to justify his defense: *I see anger in her face; she is attacking me. She said, "You guys are so smart," a sarcastic verbal attack. She said, "Let me tell you something," which is aggressive. She put the words "ditsy woman" and "stupid" in my mouth to set me up as the bad guy. When she said, "criticized by you," she accused me of being a critical person.*

This selected, biased data would be all that was available to Paul's conscious mind if he chose to take the time to review the situation. His judge would give him this rationale for defending himself: *She has attacked me, been aggressive, and falsely accused me. She is wrong. I am grossly misinterpreted and hurt. Violence is being done to my self-image as a kind and loving person.*

Note that Paul's judge did not think, *Jen's feelings have just been hurt by her boss; she wants understanding and support. I'll focus on hearing her feelings and show her that I know she is well-intentioned and competent.* These rational thoughts did not fit the judge's "bad" judgment and defend goal and so were excluded.

On the contrary, Paul's judge waxed stronger with self-defense: *Jen's attacks justify my anger!* Anger provided Paul's body with more energy to carry out the defend goal. But his clever judge realized overt anger was not socially acceptable and decided, *I'll put on a calm, rational exterior to mask my angry attack.*

So Paul verbally instructed Jen to behave properly, "Hey, calm down." He denied his attempt to correct her, "I'm not criticizing you." And he attacked her under the guise of an apparently cool, logical observation, "If you get this defensive at work, I can see how that could cause you trouble."

Jen's judge thought, *I am being misunderstood and attacked,* and she defended herself, saying, "Listen, Mister Cool, when I want your opinion on how inappropriate I am at work, I will ask. Until then, keep it to yourself." She then left the room.

Her reactions gave Paul's judge more proof: *She was sarcastic and attacking when she called me "Mr. Cool." Her saying "keep it to yourself" indicated she didn't want to hear me, to see my positive intentions or to have a close relationship with me. Her leaving the room is a rejection of me. She is not the woman to meet my needs for understanding and love.* To Paul's judge, Jen's final defensive reaction confirmed his initial "bad" judgment of her.

Jen's judge was no more rational than Paul's. Paul and Jen both ended up convinced they were right about each other's badness, and they both lost their primary love relationship. What a disaster!

Yet this pattern of thought is typical in conflict situations. Did Paul act rationally? Obviously he didn't. Does he act rationally in other situations? Yes, he does. All his friends know him as an intelligent and good-hearted person. Why on earth would he make that initial "bad" judgment against someone he loved? Conscious Paul didn't do it. *His judge did.*

On what basis does the judge make judgments? What causes the judge to discern some people or actions as good and others as bad?

Who Trained Your Judge?

Our parents provide our judges with most of their early personal training. They reward and punish us for good and bad judgments. They encourage us to look for the causes of our behavior in the external world and not to examine our own motives. We learn that we can avoid punishment and self-blame by coming up with plausible external reasons for our actions. Our judges receive additional training from babysitters, siblings, friends and from our judge's understanding of the traumatic events we may have suffered.

Our judges were raised in our families, watching TV and reading the newspaper with us. As we grew up our judges took charge of our survival. Familial and societal influences trained them to be wary of a dangerous world. For these reasons the judges of the world tend to be fearful and quick to defend.

Yet the reasons for our defensiveness go even deeper. When we were born, our judges already had a foundation. This foundation was imparted by what psychologist Dr. Carl Jung called the "collective unconscious." Where Freud saw the unconscious as containing the id's repressed wishes, Jung saw it as containing universal memory. According to Jung, man's collective unconscious "contains all the patterns of life and behavior inherited from his ancestors." The judge is a creature of habit who moves down pathways that were predetermined eons ago, in a time of survival of the fittest.

Jung referred to the collective unconscious as "a gigantic historical prejudice." This phrase explains the judge's way of thinking. Prejudice means "an adverse judgment or opinion formed beforehand without knowledge of or examination of the facts." This is how the judge operates, judging everything based on preconceived notions without taking time to test judgments or to ask questions. The judge makes the good or bad decision, within the realm of the unconscious, with finality.

The effect of the collective unconscious is evident in the shared beliefs of our society. As fish swimming in a pond hardly notice the water in which they move, we accept the world view of our social group without question. Dr. Bargh emphasizes that, "The extent to which cultural and societal norms implicitly direct our perceptions is very great."

The following experiment demonstrates how judges behave differently depending on how they were trained. At the University of Michigan, psychologists sought to determine whether Southern male students, trained under a code of honor favoring a strong response to insults, would respond differently to provocation than would Northern students, who were not raised under that code.

As they walked down the hall, individual students were bumped and insulted by an undercover experimenter. The observers of the experiment reported that the Southerners got angry and the Northerners tended to be amused. Blood tests after the incident showed significant increases of testosterone (a hormone associated with aggression) in the Southerners. The students had had the same provocation but completely different reactions, depending on where their judges were trained.

The judge, a creature of habit, learns through repetition. Dr. Bargh states that over time people develop a "chronic framework" for interpreting other people's behavior that then operates unconsciously, so that they are no longer aware of their biases.

My judge, as a result of conditioning, views the world as a fearful, hostile environment. In my culture, the world is a place of lack, threat, attack, and guilt. My judge, always frightened, triggers my anger. He tells me to attack. I yell at my son if he holds the refrigerator door open too long, I criticize the actions of people I know and of drivers on the road. I am unconscious of my judge's influence, and therefore I'm drawn into conflicts, making up reasons for my actions as my judge whirls me blindly along.

How the Judge "Sees"

Scientists used to think sight occurs in this way: the eye picks up light reflected off an object and a full image of the object is sent from the retina to the brain where it is consciously interpreted. But we now know that there is too much data coming in through our eyes for this to happen. The judge can't see and understand the whole of something quickly. Because he can't comprehend the whole picture, he has a system for making guesses. His system is machine-like and limited.

What actually happens is that in the same instant that light hits the retina, the judge automatically evaluates the fragmentary information coming in as good or bad and then characterizes it more specifically by making an approximate match from images in our unconscious memory. The image he sends to the mind is not the "real" image but more like a biased composite put together from old images. In this way the judge is actually only seeing the past projected onto the present.

Whether the nature of the image he puts together is friendly or threatening is influenced by many factors: what he expects to see, what his recent or distant associations with that type of image may be, his belief about whether the universe is friendly or unfriendly, and other influences too numerous to measure, such as whether or not he ate breakfast.

The subjective nature of the judge's image-making is easy to see in the case of someone with a different set of beliefs about the world. Take, for example, the case of a man who had lived his entire life deep in a forest that permitted visibility of only 100 yards. When he was given his first ride out of the forest onto the plain, he was convinced he saw "beetles and ants" turn into buffaloes as he was driven closer to them. They were buffaloes all the time. The reason he saw insects instead of buffaloes was that his judge arranged the visual data to suit his world view, which did not include seeing objects that were far away.

Our mood also powerfully influences what we see. When we are in a bad mood we are more likely to notice flaws. When we are in a good mood we skate over them.

The judge selects sight and sound data that confirm his judgment and establish his perception of events, people and actions. The judge freely uses stereotypes and assigns attributes such as "polite" or "rude" to ambiguous social behaviors. In this way the judge creates our psychological situation. Instead of an objective reality, we see the judge's biased projection, his patchwork interpretation of a person or event. In this way he creates our world.

Projection and Self-Fulfilling Prophecy

The thinking behind the defend goal is "I'm vulnerable and afraid; I am being attacked, and therefore I need to attack back to defend myself." The judge projects his fear and guilt onto others, then quickly blames them for victimizing him. This blaming attitude supplies the groundwork for our negative judgments, our consequent anger and our attacks on other people. Our projection makes us see attack where it does not exist.

Projecting blame onto the other person provides the excuse of self-defense, which the superego--and the world--like to see. At the psychological level, projection is a flagrant rearranging of the reality of a situation. It must remain completely unconscious to us or it wouldn't effectively resolve our inner tension, as when Jack felt free to hate and hurt Bob.

None of us would want to admit to such an unfair, infantile trick. But if something is unconscious, we don't know it is happening. So we *can't* admit it. Freud saw projection as an occasional, unconscious defense mechanism. Bargh has proven it to be the rule.

We unknowingly project and rationalize all the time. This is the judge's *spécialité de la maison*, his favorite dish to serve us. We don't know what he did to prepare it in his kitchen, but we swallow it every day, cueing the judge to serve it again.

Here is how projection created a self-fulfilling prophesy for Betsy. Betsy and Sally work in an intense, fast-paced business. Sally noticed it was about lunch time and thought of inviting Betsy, whom she hadn't gotten to know socially, to join her. Betsy was looking forward to her break at lunch and didn't want a last minute task piled on her. Sally walked into Betsy's office and Betsy's judge perceived Sally as a threat, so she said, "What is it?" with a slight edge to her voice. In a millisecond Sally's judge picked up the hard edge, felt a twinge of fear, and reversed her goal from connect to defend. So instead of inviting her to lunch, she ransacked her mind for something else to say and said, "Oh, I was just wondering if, before you left for lunch, you could make that call to the Jones account. We really need to reach them today."

Our judge, perceiving threat, defends us with a preemptive attack. When the other person responds defensively to our attack, we see their defensive act as proof of a hostile original intention. Thus Betsy's initial judgment of Sally as threatening seemed to have been proven correct. Betsy was completely unconscious of her part in influencing Sally's behavior.

We don't have to verbally attack someone to bring about the self-fulfilling prophecy. Our facial expressions and body language let the other person know how we feel. For example, the pupils in our eyes grow larger in direct proportion to our positive interest in an object or person. In one study, the greatest pupil dilation occurred in women looking at a picture of a mother and child. People automatically like faces with dilated pupils and dislike faces with constricted pupils. Bargh points out "Several studies show that people are capable of detecting the emotional expression of faces [unconsciously], and that this information influences their evaluations of [what they next see or hear.]"

But, Surely I Am Objective

Our entire lives we have believed that what we see is "real." There are three reasons why we believe that what our judge shows us is the objective truth.

First, we have no idea when we are influenced by an unconscious mental process. This is difficult for us to accept. But by definition we can *not* be conscious of the unconscious. Unconscious decision making is lightning fast and leaves no trace.

Second, we believe we see an objective reality because the judge's choices are completely convincing to us. The judge knows what we prefer to see. Why question it?

Third, the judge chooses to "see" things that others agree are there. We assume that our beliefs about people and things are the objective truth because our beliefs are commonly held by our social group, and our peers regularly validate our perceptions. But the judge is just stringing data together according to formulas that have worked in the past and are frequently inappropriate in the present. The judge prevents us from seeing people and situations as they really are.

Yet when we examine our decisions, we experience them as completely objective. If we used a process of conscious deliberation to come to the decision, then to a certain extent it is objective. There is still a problem, however. The entire information base we used to make that decision was previously selected by our judge to confirm his judgment. Because we didn't know that the data the judge gave us was biased, we trusted it.

Although the judge's use of data has a certain logic, his logic is based on a fearful child's view of the world. This means that as long as we stay within the judge's system, we cannot be objective. Dr. Bargh states, "We experience the output of these preconscious analyses as if these meanings and understandings were clearly present in the objective world, when in fact they are not."

It is difficult to face this lack of objectivity, even in the face of scientific proof. Dr. Bargh describes how hard it is to get someone to understand this:

> Anyone who has ever attempted to explain to a lay friend or relative that mental events can occur and affect their judgments and behavior without their knowing about it can attest that it is a difficult task indeed. What even the best-intentioned and open-minded individual will do when confronted with such an idea is to examine their autobiographical memory, find no cases in which they were influenced without knowing it (of course!), and reply, "Uh-uh, not me, Jack."

We like to think that we are conscious. We hate to admit we are wrong. The Freudian theory of resistance states that we don't understand what we don't want to understand. We don't want to understand that we operate unconsciously. Yet, according to the scientists, we are unconscious ninety-nine percent of the time.

It's frightening to think we haven't got the control over our lives we thought we had.

We don't know exactly how the judge's unconscious thoughts occur in the mind. They happen at lightning speed, apparently simultaneously, and completely outside our awareness. But from what scientists have been able to measure and from intelligent guesses based on people's behavior, here is a suggested model summarizing the judge's tasks is presented in Table 3.

Table 3 – **The Judge's Tasks**

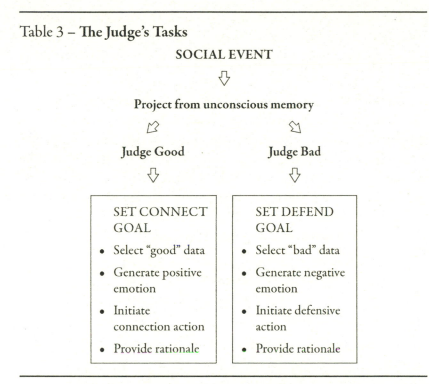

SOCIAL EVENT

⇩

Project from unconscious memory

↗   ↖

Judge Good   **Judge Bad**

⇩   ⇩

SET CONNECT GOAL	SET DEFEND GOAL
• Select "good" data	• Select "bad" data
• Generate positive emotion	• Generate negative emotion
• Initiate connection action	• Initiate defensive action
• Provide rationale	• Provide rationale

Desi and the Prince: The Judge Personified in Literature

This classic story depicts a judge's insidious destruction of a relationship.

Desi was a talented, happy, and very beautiful young woman. She was much sought after by the most eligible men in the splendid capital city in which she lived.

One day her father invited a prince, who was a famous military commander, to visit. While the prince told his war stories to her father, Desi sat off to the side listening. Over the duration of his many visits to her father, Desi got to know all about the prince's fascinating life, and also his personality. She came to deeply appreciate his noble character, his modesty and self-restraint, and the respect he showed to other people. She fell in love with him, and they eloped. They were wonderfully happy.

Shortly after their wedding Desi joined the prince on a military campaign. They went with two of the prince's officers, his trusted aide-de-camp, "honest Iago," and his lieutenant, Cassio, who was a friend of Desi's.

Almost immediately the prince began acting irrationally toward Desi. First he complained of a headache. Then he berated her for misplacing a handkerchief, and, not long after that, for no apparent reason, he struck her and ordered her out of his sight. Later he demanded to know if she had been faithful to him. She said "yes" but he didn't believe her and called her a whore. In their bedroom he accused her of sleeping with one of his officers. She denied it, but he refused to believe her, and, in a rage, killed her.

Shortly thereafter the prince found out he had been completely mistaken, that Desi really had been faithful to him all along. He was so deeply stricken with remorse for killing his wife, whom he loved very much, that he killed himself.

What caused him to behave in such an irrational way?

The prince's name was Othello. This play by William Shakespeare has been famous for four hundred years for some excellent reasons. One is that people can identify with Desdemona (Desi) and with Othello. We all know how agonizing it can be to have others misunderstand us and get angry with us for no apparent reason. And we can also identify with the prince: getting angry with someone we love and then feeling sad when we realize we made a mistake.

What makes the play *Othello* so pertinent to our understanding of the unconscious is the character responsible for Othello's irrational behavior, his judge, Iago. Iago is the unconscious personified. Shakespeare has given us a clear picture of how Iago influences Othello's thinking. Although he has an "honest" exterior to Othello, the audience gets to see Iago's fearful thoughts:

- *I may be of humble origins, but I have had a great deal of military experience. I am furious that Othello promoted the less experienced, upper-class Cassio over me to the rank of lieutenant.*

- *I feel inferior to and jealous of Othello and Cassio.*

- *I want to possess Desdemona.*

- *I fear that Othello may have slept with my wife.* [This thought indicates that Iago has projected his own desire to sleep with another man's wife onto Othello.]

Iago deliberately plans to destroy them by introducing suspicions "to abuse Othello's ear." Iago sets the stage by persuading Cassio to drink too much and get into a fight, which results in Othello demoting him. Iago then prompts Cassio to ask Desdemona to plead to Othello for his reinstatement. Desdemona agrees to do this for her friend.

The stage now set, Iago begins to color Othello's thoughts by telling him that he sees Cassio acting guilty about something. Iago pours "pestilence" in Othello's ear. He insinuates that Desdemona lusts for Cassio and that they have been having an affair. The first jealous thoughts seize Othello.

Iago goes on to lead Othello "by the nose," telling him, "Look to your wife; observe her well with Cassio."

By now, Desdemona has begun pleading to Othello to reinstate Cassio as lieutenant. But Iago has so warped Othello's thinking that he interprets her pleading as an attempt to gain advancement for her lover. The more Desdemona pleads to Othello to reinstate Cassio, the more Othello suspects that she has been unfaithful.

Iago reminds Othello that Desdemona deceived her father when she eloped, so deceit is in her nature. As a clincher, Iago tells Othello, who is black, that Desdemona would naturally prefer a man of her own complexion.

Finally, Iago "proves" Desdemona's infidelity to Othello. He swipes a handkerchief from Desdemona, which Othello had given her, and plants it on Cassio. When Othello sees that Cassio now has this love token he is convinced of her guilt. Iago's comment, "Trifles light as air are to the jealous confirmations strong as proofs of holy writ," demonstrates his understanding that a jealous mind finds what it is looking for. Othello, convinced he has been betrayed, kills Desdemona.

This classic tragedy speaks to all of us. Why are people drawn to tragedy as an art form? In a tragedy "the main character is brought to ruin or suffers extreme sorrow... as a consequence of a tragic flaw, a moral weakness or an inability to cope with unfavorable circumstances." Many of us identify with tragedies because, when a conflict occurs that affects our well-being and we most need to do or say the right thing, our internal judges take over and we self-sabotage. This is no idle concern. Your judge is an integral, unconscious part of you, leading you to tremendous pain and loss over a lifetime. *Your judge is your tragic flaw.*

The Judge Rules the Realm

Our judge primes our thoughts in the same way Iago primed Othello. When we are afraid, our judge takes control of our personalities. The result is damaged and lost relationships.

We can see the devastation wrought on a wider scale. Here are examples of the judge's power in the world:

- More than half of all marriages end in divorce. Many of those who remain married are unhappy. A frightening lack of intimacy is the model for our children.

- People are afraid at the workplace. They feel threatened, coerced, disrespected and therefore unable to be themselves. They are consequently unable to be creative, productive, or happy at work.

- Most men don't have good friendships. They isolate, even with their partners. They rely desperately on performance-based esteem. Most of them are unable to express their feelings. These pent-up feelings finally burst out in rage and violence. Our prison population is booming, with the highest per capita rate of incarceration in the world.

- Women receive the brunt of the physical violence and shoulder the added child-rearing responsibilities. Yet they have judges too, leading them to sabotage their own attempts at forming happy relationships.

- A great many people in America lack self-esteem, self-confidence, and inner peace. They use mind-altering drugs, alcohol, work, sex, and TV to avoid the pain of not loving themselves and not being able to relate positively to others.

Actually, learning that we have a judge is good news. Yes, we have been operating unconsciously, but we couldn't do anything about it because we didn't know it. Now that we know what the judge does, we can free ourselves from the tyranny of the unconscious and find happiness in our relationships.

We are not our judges. Our judges are our servants, not our masters. We can wake up and regain our power. Interacting with people can become a constant source of personal and professional satisfaction. *We have everything we need to transform conflict into connection.*

A Human Being is a part of the whole called by us universe, a part limited in time and space. He experiences himself, his thoughts and feelings as something separated from the rest, a kind of optical delusion of consciousness. This delusion is a kind of prison for us, restricting us to our personal desires and to affection for a few persons nearest us. Our task must be to free ourselves from this prison by widening our circle of compassion to embrace all living creatures...

– ALBERT EINSTEIN

CHAPTER FOUR

Harmonious Resolution

We can break out of prison and correct our judge's mistakes. We can even learn to see them coming and prevent them, turning our interactions with people into positive connections. We can save our relationships. It is never too late.

Can we control or influence the unconscious so we can be more accurate in our judgments, more able to understand and get along with other people? Here is the story of how Sylvia changed the way she related to one of her employees at a busy hospital. First, you will see her judge in action. Then, after Sylvia consciously overrides her judge, you will see how she creates a harmonious resolution.

Sylvia and Tom Confront Each Other

Sylvia, the director of nursing for a busy medical unit, was uneasy. On the previous day a crisis had occurred at shift change and a patient had almost died. Everyone in the unit was shaken. Sylvia called a staff meeting to talk about it. She wondered if Tom, the head of technical services, might give her some trouble as he had on previous occasions. As she opened the meeting, she first briefly reviewed the recent events and then asked the group, "What can we do to prevent a crisis like this from happening again?"

Tom looked right at her and in a loud voice said, "What can we do? Let me tell you something. If *you* ever got off your office chair and came out on the floor to do your job, crises like this wouldn't happen."

Dead silence. Everyone wondered how Sylvia would defend herself. Her judge reacted in a fraction of a second. If made conscious, her judge's thoughts and feelings would have sounded like this:

Tom's really mad and blaming me. I'm afraid. He's challenging my competence in front of my staff. I feel embarrassed. But I'm the director and I do a good job. Just who does he think he is? I'm angry. I need to show that he's wrong and get myself out of this embarrassing situation.

So she said to him, "You have no right to criticize me. I called this meeting to get cooperation solving a serious problem. If you're just going to attack me you can leave right now."

"No, I'm not going to leave!" replied Tom, "I'll tell you what the 'serious problem' is; it's lazy managers who only care about their privileges and don't give a damn about what's happening out there on the floor. We're dealing with life and death situations while you sit in your cushy office with the door closed. Well we are fed up with it. I've talked to the others and they feel the same way. We're going to tell the medical director just what's going on here."

Sylvia and Tom usually confronted each other in exactly this way. Each time it proved to be a disaster. The rest of the staff and the patients also felt the negative fallout from these attacks, which created a tense environment in the unit.

In this interaction, Sylvia made a mistake. She let her fear rule and went along with her judge. Her judge evaluated Tom as bad and gave her information about Tom's red face, his staring eyes and his loud words. This was all she could see because of her judge's negative judgment and defend goal. Understandably, she perceived him as attacking her.

Notice that her judge didn't give her conscious mind any information about Tom feeling frightened by the patient's near death, desperately wanting help, but feeling embarrassed to ask for it. Nor did her judge tell her that people who are in pain and desperately want help often sound as if they are attacking.

Sylvia unknowingly accepted the judge's version—that Tom's primary intention was to attack her, and she defended herself by asking him to leave. Asking him to leave was the opposite of what she had originally hoped, which was to get his cooperation to prevent another crisis. Although Sylvia had good intentions, her judge sabotaged her efforts.

When we have a negative impression of someone, we are unlikely to question it so our judge's automatic judgment determines that we get off to a negative start with them. Once started, the judge's automatic processes keep us headed in a negative direction.

We can overcome our automatic judgments. We can learn to become aware that we are making them, choose to discount them, and seek more accurate information. In this way we see people more truthfully and have better interactions with them. Here is how Sylvia did this with Tom.

Sylvia Connects with Tom

Prior to this confrontation with Tom, Sylvia participated in a conscious communication training workshop and, by using the tools of conscious communication, she was able to hear and respond differently to Tom. Watch how Sylvia handles Tom this time.

Sylvia opened the meeting by briefly reviewing yesterday's events and then asked the group "What can we do to prevent a crisis like this from happening again?"

Tom looked right at her and in a loud voice said: "What can we do? Let me tell you something. If *you* ever got off your office chair and came out on the floor to do your job, crises like this wouldn't happen."

Sylvia was immediately aware of feeling mad at Tom. So she paused briefly to put aside her judge's defensive judgment and chose instead to find out for herself what was going on inside Tom. She said, "Tom, it sounds like you're really angry about what happened yesterday."

"You bet I am! And I'm not alone."

"Are you upset because you want greater clarity about who's supposed to do what?"

"No. You don't even know how desperate the situation is out there. I have eighty thousand things to do at shift change and patients' lives are at stake."

"So you're really stressed at those times and afraid for the patients' safety?"

"Yes, but this place is totally unfair. We're understaffed and asked to do the impossible."

"That sounds really frustrating. So would you like to find a way you could get the support you need to provide a safe transition at shift change?"

"I sure would."

"I want you to have the support you need, Tom. Tell me more about it."

Tom did tell her about it. As Sylvia listened, Tom cooled down. After a while they came up with a positive solution that worked for both of them.

This approach is different from what we are used to. By stopping and shifting her thinking, Sylvia ignored her judge's automatic negative judgment of Tom and was then able to effectively listen to him. She guessed at what he was feeling and what his positive unmet intentions might be. She found that behind his angry words and his confrontational style, Tom was asking for help. He cared strongly about providing safe care for the patients and was upset about the near death.

The underlying intention behind Tom's behavior was not attack. He was in pain and calling for help, albeit in a manner that could easily be interpreted as attack. When a person against whom our judge holds a prejudice is upset and calls for help, *our judge sees the call for help as an attack.*

After Sylvia had listened to and understood Tom, she proceeded to work with him and the rest of the staff as they formed a plan for better coverage during shift change. Both ended up feeling pleased with the solution and better about their relationship with each other. Notice that only Sylvia needed to know how to communicate effectively in order to bring about a happy resolution for Tom and herself.

It is a psychological fact that our judge always speaks first. He judges before we know it and his judgments are frequently inaccurate and negative. The only way we are likely to become aware of them is when we realize we are angry with someone. This is a golden moment. In this instant, we can become conscious. Noticing our upset feeling is our "alarm" that the judge has made a negative judgment; and we can use this alarm to wake up.

If our emotion is any form of upset, our judge has made a "bad" judgment. Now we can choose to find out what is really going on inside the other person and make a positive connection.

Choose Conscious Override

We can take control back from our judge with our conscious mind. Psychologists refer to this as the "conscious override" of automatic, unconscious behavior. Conscious override allows us to ignore the negatively-biased sense data selected by our judges and to choose, instead, to find more accurate, positive data. This allows us to see the situation differently and to understand people instead of judging and attacking them.

Imagine you work in a hospital ward for children afflicted with a disease that causes their muscles to jerk unpredictably. Walking is hard for them and they fall down a lot, but they improve with practice. You like the kids and encourage them to walk. One day one of the kids you're helping starts to fall and on the way down her arm smacks you a good one in the face. Your judge is instantly enraged at being struck. But your conscious mind knows the child hadn't the least intention of hitting you and, so, you discount your anger. You correct yourself. Your anger lasts only a fraction of a second. You forget it, smile, and bend down to help the child.

Imagine that a little while later an adult bumps you out in the hall and doesn't say, "excuse me." You become angry, but this time you don't discount your anger. Why? Because you accept your judge's decision, that the other person is self-centered, uncaring, and old enough to know proper etiquette. Your anger seems justified, so you don't bother to reevaluate it.

Let's take it one more step. Imagine that you stop the person, say "Ouch, that hurt," and make eye contact.

The other person seems to come back to awareness from some far-off place and says, "Oh, I'm terribly sorry; I wasn't paying any attention; my little boy just died in the cancer ward."

Suddenly you see this person differently and reevaluate your self-righteous stance. You see they didn't mean to hurt you. You forget about the bump and are no longer angry. On the contrary, you empathize with them.

The way we look at a situation determines how we feel about it. At each shift in the story we saw how changing our mind about the other person's motive changed how we saw and interacted with them. When our thinking about the person changed, we shifted from pursuing the defend goal to the connect goal.

What is alarming is how seldom we consciously choose to find out what is going on inside another person. We content ourselves with the judge's superficial interpretation.

Using conscious override requires a choice, *to not believe what our eyes and ears tell us*. In doing this we revoke our judge's complete control. It bears repeating: we are not our judge.

Who are we if we are not the judge? First of all, we are conscious. We are aware that we have thoughts and feelings. We are the witnesses or observers. As Dr. Susan S. Trout, Executive Director of the Institute for Attitudinal Studies, poetically put it:

> I have a body, but I am not my body. I am more than that.
> My body may be in different conditions of health or sickness.
> It may be rested or tired, but it is not my real "I."
> My body is my precious instrument of experience and of action,
> but it is not my self.
> I have a body, but I am not my body. I am more than that.
> I am the one who is aware.
>
> I have emotions, but I am more than my emotions.
> They are countless and contradictory, changing,
> And yet I know that I always remain I, my self,
> In a state of irritation or calm.
> Since I can observe, understand and judge my
> Emotions and then increasingly dominate, direct
> And utilize them, it is evident that they are not my self.
> I have emotions, but I am not my emotions. I am more than that.
> I am the one who is aware.

I have an intellect, but I am more than my intellect.
It may be quiet or active.
It is capable of expanding, letting go of limiting beliefs and learning new attitudes.
It is an organ of knowledge in regard to the inner world as well as the outer. But it is not my self.
I have an intellect, but I am not my intellect. I am more than that.
I am the one who is aware.

I am the center of pure awareness,
I am a center of will,
Capable of mastering and directing all my energies:
Physical, emotional, mental and spiritual.
I am the one who is aware.
I am the self.

How can we make use of our awareness? Teacher of meditation Ram Dass speaks of distinguishing our conscious self from our unconscious judge in this way:

We see that we need not identify with each thought just because it happens to occur. We can remain calm and choose which thought we wish to attend to. And we can remain aware behind all these thoughts, in a state that offers an entirely new level of openness and insight.

Another meditation teacher says,

We dis-identify by observing. Instead of being absorbed by sensations, feelings, desires, thoughts, we observe them objectively without judging them, without wanting to change them, without interfering with them in any way. We see them as distinct from us, as if we were looking at a landscape.

The attitude of serene observation can be practiced at any moment of our life, and its first effect is that of liberation. I am fearful, I observe my fear, I see its contours clearly, I see that the fear is not me, that it is a thing outside myself; I am free of that fear.

We have free will but we haven't known how to choose the thoughts we entertain. The ability to consciously override our unwanted reactions is directly linked to health, happiness and success.

Our attitudes guide our thoughts. When the judge's negative judgment kicks the defend goal into gear, his attitude about other people is: "*The other person is wrong and has a bad intention.*" This attitude guides his sorting of the data coming in through the senses.

Now that we've exposed the judge's game, what is the alternative? Using our adult ability to reason, we first reject the judge's harmful assumptions about scarcity. Freudian psychology is fear-based and pessimistic. We need a new paradigm.

There is enough to go around. Since Freud, a new optimistic school of psychology has arisen—humanistic psychology. Dr. Abraham Maslow posited that people have a natural drive to self-actualize. Maslow made a distinction between deficiency-based and sufficiency-based motives. When we fear scarcity, as the judge does, we enter relationships with a desire to get something.

On the other hand, when we have a sense of wholeness and well-being, we enter relationships with a desire to share and to enhance the relationship. We know from our own experience that when we are happy and fulfilled, our relationships flow more easily, bringing us greater satisfaction.

Our essential goodness is just waiting to be heard and understood. Carl Rogers expressed it beautifully:

It has been my experience that persons have a basically positive direction...

If I can create a relationship characterized on my part:

> by a genuineness and transparency, in which I am my real feelings;
>
> by a warm acceptance of and prizing of the other person as a separate individual;
>
> by a sensitive ability to see his world and himself as he sees them;

Then the other individual in the relationship:

> will experience and understand aspects of himself which previously he has repressed;
>
> will find himself becoming better integrated, more able to function effectively;
>
> will become more similar to the person he would like to be;
>
> will be more self-directing and self-confident;
>
> will become more of a person, more unique and more self-expressive;
>
> will be more understanding, more acceptant of others;
>
> will be able to cope with problems of life more adequately and more comfortably.

This has also been my experience as a listener. As I accept another person, they feel the satisfaction of being heard and understood. Connection soothes them and transforms them; they are now free to move ahead and to change. And I feel better too. Connection heals both of us.

When we consciously override our negative judgment we quickly realize the relational abundance around us and begin to treat people kindly. We then show them the "unconditional positive regard" described by Carl Rogers.

When we are in a conflict with someone, our judge is enraged with theirs. When we choose to connect with the good in them, however, the other person's conscious self notices our positive regard and welcomes it. Then, without even realizing it, they override their own judge in order to have their goodness understood and accepted by us.

To see the good in people we need to be able to tell the difference between what the judge wants and what people want. Because our judge's world view is based on his assumptions of scarcity and competition, he feels a rush of satisfaction when he wins something monetary or blames someone for something. The "pleasure" experienced from either of these is short-lived.

Judge Specificity

Judge thinking is immature and therefore concrete rather than abstract. The judge wants specific objects or actions to satisfy immediate needs. *I want chocolate ice cream. I want Larry to clean the garage. I want $20,000 to buy a new car.* When these thoughts occur, the judge can become fixed on them and put up psychological blinders to other means of satisfaction. *No, I don't want vanilla. Larry better not beg off. $12,000 isn't enough.* And the judge experiences frustration if these specifics are unavailable.

Judges fail to realize they are often setting themselves up for disappointment with such narrow wants. Not only might the specific thing be unavailable, it may not bring satisfaction even when it is attained. Perhaps the desire for chocolate ice cream was based on feeling tired or lonely. Wanting Larry to clean the garage might be just a symptom of desiring more joyful cooperation in an intimate partnership. And the personal need for a specific sum of money may be based on a wish for security that money can never satisfy.

Individuals with incomes ranging from $12,000 to $250,000, responding to a random survey, all had one thing in common—that their current income wasn't quite enough to make ends meet. When asked what would satisfy them, they each stated an income 50% greater than their current income.

Contrast this with the fact that Americans' per-person income, *after* adjusting for inflation, is *more than double* what it was in 1957. Yet since that time, the number of Americans who say they are "very happy" has *declined* from 35 to 30 percent.

Money, apparently, doesn't bring happiness. When we accept the judge's specific, fixed thinking, we are setting ourselves up for fears of scarcity. The judge is short-sighted and doesn't know what brings true, lasting happiness.

Human Hopes

If we set the judge aside, how specific can we get about what people really want? In our stories, Tom, Sylvia and Jen all wanted to be perceived as competent and to have their thoughts and feelings respected. These are *freedom* hopes. Tom wanted to be heard, understood and supported by Sylvia. Sylvia wanted support and cooperation from Tom. Jen wanted to be heard and understood by Paul. These are all hopes for *connection*.

Human hopes fall into these two broad categories: freedom and connection. Table 4 lists our common hopes.

In a relational sense, our freedom hopes are about being perceived by others as good. Maslow writes that, "We all want to be recognized and accepted for what we are in our fullness, richness and complexity," and we resist and rage at being quickly categorized by another person.

In a relationship, *our hopes for freedom need to be balanced with our hopes for connection*. Sometimes we want to be close with another person and sometimes we want to be free to do something our way. If we listen to our judge, our attempts to balance freedom and connection lead to conflict. However, if we override our judge and connect with the other person, we not only resolve conflict, we can also meet our hopes for freedom.

An important thing to notice about our hopes is that they are abstract rather than specific. They represent higher values. Being abstract, there is no scarcity; they can be met in a variety of ways. Meeting a hope is therefore never dependent on a single person or event. If one person isn't in the mood to hear and understand us, we can find someone who is.

When our hopes are all met, we experience peace of mind. This is our goal, our highest value. Peace of mind can be sought through prayer and meditation, but in my experience, it can be found most directly

---

Table 4 – Our Hopes

FREEDOM HOPES	CONNECTION HOPES
to have our own thoughts and opinions	to be heard and understood
to have our own feelings	to have our thoughts considered by others
to have our own intentions	to be accepted by others
to choose how we will spend our time	to be appreciated
to have our own values	to experience harmony with others
to have our own dreams, goals and aspirations	to experience closeness and intimacy
to say what we think and feel	to be supported
to express our creativity	to be trusted
to experience privacy, order and psychological safety	to love and be loved
to be treated with honesty	to experience communion
to be respected	to help others get their hopes met

---

by changing our thinking about other people, by making the shift from defense to connection.

We could add wholeness, integrity, and meaning to our list of hopes; they span both categories. Anything that is a good, abstract quality can be put on the list.

Spiritually inclined people refer to hopes as aspects of love, or as divine or holy attributes. This is advantageous in linking hopes into a broader, reinforcing belief system. Looking at hopes as aspects of love is optional. In order to use them powerfully we only need to understand that they are the good intentions inside all of us. Because we are all essentially the same, we all want the same abstract qualities; we all share the same hopes.

Even the judge, for all his fearful short-sightedness, has his eye on hopes. When he judges something "bad" he sees it as threatening his hopes. His mistake is in seeing them threatened when they are not, and in substituting false hopes such as having money and assigning blame.

We can never get our hopes met at anyone else's expense. To do so would negate our own hopes for connection. This is why forcing or coercing another person does not bring happiness, which is found only through mutual cooperation. For this reason, self-sacrifice is a useless endeavor. Given the interconnectedness of hopes, *either we both get our hopes met or neither of us does.* My being heard and understood doesn't mean there is less opportunity for you. Actually the opposite is true. If you hear and understand me, I feel better and am more ready to listen and empathize with you.

All our hopes are always present, but we feel the need for different hopes at various times; generally, we are not even aware of a hope until we suddenly think it is missing or about to be lost. This could happen when our judge sees someone as depriving us. It occurred to Sylvia when her judge interpreted Tom's words as intentional attacks and she became angry.

Our Happiness Is Linked to Our Goals

Lasting happiness requires that both connection and freedom hopes are met. When our judge causes conflict, however, our connection hopes are lost. So, to avoid conflict, many of us have done what we thought we "should" or "had to" do in order to get along with others. We changed our behavior, but not our mind, and we still failed to connect. Why? Because when we did what we didn't want to do, we felt coerced and, therefore, angry. Our behavior was not genuine and other people saw through us.

> *The only way to find lasting peace and happiness is to change our goal to connection with freedom. This brings love and respect together. To respect a loved one's freedom is to truly love them. This is what we all want to give and receive.*

The program presented here is practical and action-oriented. As we use conscious override we discover that people are essentially the same as we are. As we look for good intention, we will find it. I know this because, as I have worked with hundreds of people over many years, I have found one fact about people to be universally true: *we are always doing our best to get our hopes met.* People are always pursuing a hope, no matter how unskillfully.

Given this understanding, our guiding attitude toward other people becomes, "*You have a good intention and I want to find it.*" Stepping outside of the judge's fearful control and opening our senses to gather new information allows us to connect with others.

Psychologists Roy Baumeister, Todd Heatherton, and Diane Tice describe conscious override in their book, *Losing Control: How and Why People Fail at Self-Regulation.* They say: "When people are able to think beyond the immediate situation and interpret events with reference to [higher values, they are] able to exert substantial control over themselves and override many impulses."

Not Guilty!

Sometimes in trying to get a hope met we make a mistake. If Bill had known a car was going to block his path, he wouldn't have pulled out, endangering his son and the pick-up truck driver. But he didn't know. His attempt to meet his hope of buying a toy for his son was not malicious. He was merely mistaken in his timing.

We all make mistakes. Boy, do we ever. We don't mean to. Given another chance to get our hope met without making a mistake, without hurting someone else, we would do it. Making social mistakes means that, while trying to meet one hope, we've confounded our hope of helping others.

In these instances we are not morally guilty and neither is the other person. Certainly we need to exercise care around someone in the grip of his judge. But in the words of Mary Wollstonecraft Shelly, "No man consciously chooses evil because it is evil; he only mistakes it for the happiness he seeks."

When... someone really hears you without passing judgment on you, without trying to take responsibility for you, without trying to mold you, it feels darn good. ...When I have been listened to and when I have been heard, I am able to reperceive my world in a new way and to go on. It is astonishing how elements which seem insoluble become soluble when someone listens. How confusions which seemed irremediable turn into relatively clear flowing streams when one is heard.

– CARL ROGERS

CHAPTER FIVE

Empathic Listening

After a long day Michael, a recently divorced father, dropped into his favorite chair and opened the newspaper, whereupon his son, Joey, shouted,

"I hate you! I want to spend all my time at Mom's house from now on."

Michael put the paper down, "I've had it. She's been telling you I'm a bad person, hasn't she? What did she say?"

"She didn't say anything."

Michael shifted course, "Come on, Joey, you like it here. Didn't I just get you a new bicycle?"

"That bicycle stinks! I hate it here! I want to go home, right now!"

Scenes like this occurred on each of Joey's visits to Michael's new apartment. Michael was going nuts before he came to a parent education class. Imagine Michael had responded using conscious listening skills:

This time when Joey says, "I hate you. I want to spend all my time at Mom's from now on," Michael takes a breath, looks at him, and says, "Joey, when I sit down to read the paper, do you feel angry because you want some attention?"

Joey just pushes his lips together, so Michael adds, "Would you like me to put the paper away and play with you?"

After a brief pause Joey says, "Let's play Monopoly®."

"Well come over here and let's talk about it," Michael replies, holding out his arms. He pulls Joey up on his lap and in a few seconds they're wrestling and laughing.

Joey's words, "I hate you!" expressed his anger but not what he was really wanting—connection. Michael was particularly frustrated by Joey's words because he wanted to be understood as a caring father. But before he could gain the rewards of being understood he needed to learn an important sequence.

When people are upset, like Joey, they are out of balance, off center. Their judges are in control. They need to be heard and brought back to center before they will be able to hear us. And *before* we can do this we need to override our own judge's screams for instant gratification and bring ourselves back to center. Putting our own needs temporarily on hold is a personal challenge that requires our conscious attention. Here are four ways to center ourselves, which can be used singly or in combination.

Centering

1. Breathing: Take a deep, slow breath into the lower lobes of your lungs. This has an immediate calming effect.

2. Physical Centering: Feel your feet solidly on the ground. Put your conscious attention on your physical center, a point two inches below your navel. Breathe into this spot, feel power flowing through you, and relax.

3. Mantra: Repeat a short phrase silently to yourself such as "I am peaceful and strong" or "Nothing can harm me."

4. Visualization: Give an image to your own need and put that image in brackets. [My need on hold.] It will be right there waiting for you once your listening has returned the other person to center.

Often when we try to listen to others we miss the boat because our judge doesn't know how to find out what is going on inside the other person. Our judge decides in a flash and pursues that judgment. When the other person perceives that they have been judged, they become upset.

The Two-edged Sword

Carl pulled his scarf a little tighter as he walked past the library toward the student union. In the fading light of the Wisconsin winter he saw Helen waiting for him. She smiled as he approached, her face highlighted against her dark blue collar, which was dusted with snowflakes. They went inside, got hot chocolates, and Carl led her to a table off to the side, behind the Rathskellar's heavy arches.

"I had a fight with my roommate today," Helen said. "She ate some of the food my mother sent me. When I found out I was so mad. I don't know why it felt like such a big deal."

"What'd you do?"

"I told her not to do it again, but I felt hot in the face and nervous. I couldn't keep my voice steady. Sometimes I feel so weak, like I'm hypersensitive and fragile. It's embarrassing." She shifted on her chair. "So how'd your religion seminar go this morning?"

"I survived."

"Survived! What happened?"

"The professor said my paper failed to explain Wycliffe's rejection of transubstantiation."

"To explain what?"

"He basically said I didn't know my facts, that I was just writing down my own ideas."

"I see," replied Helen gently. "Then what?"

"Then this snide little guy, Williams, jumped in and said that I should have footnoted the sources of my ideas. He implied I was cheating and using other people's stuff."

"Oh, no!" She put her hand on his.

Carl looked down at the snow melting off his boot.

Helen put a little pressure on his hand. "How do you feel?"

"Damn that little jerk! What does he know about it? He was just trying to make me look bad in front of everybody."

"That must have been awful!"

Carl turned his head around to the side. After a minute he picked up his napkin and wiped the corners of his eyes.

"You must think I'm really childish," he said.

"No, not at all." She waited, then added, "I know how much your integrity means to you. And I know how much work you put in on that paper." He looked back at her.

"Carl, thanks for telling me."

He wrapped his fingers around her hand and gave it a squeeze. "I'm a little embarrassed," he said.

"Yeah, and I feel closer to you," she said, smiling.

He raised her hand to his lips and held it there, looking steadily into her eyes.

They married a few years later. Carl switched fields, eventually becoming a psychologist. His partnership with Helen was an enduring source of happiness and strength. It gave him the courage to be authentic and vulnerable in his professional life. At his death in 1987, Carl Rogers had become the most influential psychologist in America, the man who taught the world the power of empathic listening.

Empathic listening involves entering another person's world nonjudgmentally and accepting their feelings and meanings. Although the words of the above exchange are imaginary, they illustrate the empathic listening for which Carl and Helen were noted. Helen was being empathic when she asked Carl, "How do you feel?" and when she said, "That must have been awful."

Empathy is necessary in a healthy relationship. Yet in spite of our knowledge of the healing power of empathic listening, our relationships are falling apart and our divorce rate is climbing. At a basic level something is still terribly wrong. Empathy, as understood and taught by Carl Rogers and those who have followed him, is a two-edged sword. It can act in a positive direction or in a negative one. Empathizing with negative meanings is easy to do, and it results in situations like the following:

Lean and affable, Matt Wagner was the top salesman for Charlton Office Furniture. The company was expanding and hired a new sales manager, Doug Harris. Two weeks after Doug became his manager, Matt came home to his wife, Donna, and said,

"I had a lousy day."

"What happened?"

"Doug told me to use the new audio-visual sales aid in my pitch. I told him I didn't want to because it cramps my style."

"What'd he say."

"He told me to get with the program and use it."

"That must be frustrating. Are you worried that he's going to mess up your sales?"

"Maybe, because that's not all. He said I had to write my sales reports immediately after each sales call, right there in my car before I leave the parking lot. That takes a lot of prime time. I wonder if he's trying to slow me down."

"Slow you down! What does he know? You're the best salesman they've got. There's no one in that company standing up for you. I wish you worked for people who appreciated you."

Within a week Matt had accepted a job at another office furniture company. But as part of his termination with Charlton, he had to go to back for an exit interview.

After the interview Matt came home and said to Donna, "Well, that was a surprise."

"Was Doug there?"

"No. It was Ed, the Human Resources guy. But he said Doug was real upset that I quit."

"Really?"

"Yeah. I guess Doug wanted me to do the write-ups right after each call so I'd remember the details. He wanted to share the way I handled objections with the rest of the sales force."

"Well, why didn't he say that?"

"I don't know. And I guess that sales aid is effective. Now I'm not so sure... I'm not looking forward to the extra travel to this new job."

"Maybe you should have stayed."

"For crying out loud! You're the one who told me to quit!"

Matt resented Donna for months, largely because she had empathized with his negative ideas about Doug. This story illustrates two common problems.

The first is the misperception that occurs with unconscious judgment. Matt perceived Doug's requests to use the sales aid and to write up his reports as threats to his sales income. Later he learned that Doug's intention was to help him become even more effective.

The second common problem the story illustrates is the danger of empathizing with a person's negative thinking. Donna empathized with Matt's suspicion that Doug was trying to slow him down. By doing this she inadvertently increased Matt's fear. He thought she was implying that a new job was his best course of action. After he quit, and it didn't appear to be such a good idea, he resented Donna. This problem of empathizing with negative thinking happens frequently and leads people into conflicts.

Both problems wreak havoc with our relationships and, with all due respect to his tremendous contribution, Carl Rogers had no solution. That is because the true nature of the problems and their solutions was not understood until the powerful influence exerted by the unconscious on our thinking was discovered.

An example of a better way for Donna to empathize with Matt would have been to ask "Are you concerned because you want to keep your sales high?" This slight rewording makes a big difference because it aims Matt's thinking in a positive direction.

How the Judge Listens

To experience how people typically listen, imagine this situation. One morning you arrive at work and your manager asks you to do something for him. He needs it done by 5:00 p.m. You plan to do it right away but an emergency comes up that takes your full attention. Another emergency follows the first one; the day becomes frantically busy and you forget all about what the manager asked you to do.

At the end of the day, as you're about to leave for home with some other employees, your manager walks up to you and requests the work he'd asked for. You start to explain about the emergencies.

He cuts you off and says loudly: "I don't give a damn. I pay you to get work done, not to muck around."

You start to reply, but he interrupts, "Save your excuses."

Then he turns his back and leaves. The other employees pretend not to have heard. You're quite upset and, rather than go straight home, you stop at your friend Joan's house and tell her the whole story.

Imagine that Joan replies in the following ways. Read each reply aloud and pause to notice how you feel hearing it.

1. "Don't let it bother you. It was just a misunderstanding. There's no reason to take it so hard."

2. "How awful! You must be devastated. You poor thing. I feel so sorry for you."

3. "Here's what you can do. Go in early and finish the work. Then admit to your manager that you slipped up and let him know you won't forget his requests in the future."

4. "It's important to get top-priority work done on time."

5. "You think that's bad. Do you know what my old boss did to me? He told me to 'shape up or ship out' in front of the whole office!"

6. "Didn't you understand the importance of what he wanted? How could you forget it? Have you done things like this before? Why didn't you stay late and finish it?"

7. "I can see why he'd be upset. Managers need to be able to count on employees to carry out their requests."

8. "You're really bringing this up to make a statement about the company's leadership."

9. "You're upset because you see your boss as another victimizer. When you were a child you saw yourself as a victim of your father's anger and now your manager is reminding you of your father. That's why you're so afraid of him."

Table 5 shows what was probably occurring unconsciously in Joan:

Table 5 – **Summary of Judge Listening Techniques**

JOAN'S WORDS	HER JUDGE'S THINKING
"Don't let it bother you. It was just a misunderstanding. There's no reason to take it so hard."	Joan's judge is uncomfortable with your emotion and is attempting to avoid discomfort by denying your feelings and minimizing the incident.
"How awful! You must be devastated. You poor thing. I feel so sorry for you."	Her judge is assuming that you are incapable of getting your needs met. Her judge is projecting self-pity onto you in the form of sympathy.
"Here's what you can do. Go in early and finish the work. Then admit to your manager that you slipped up and let him know you won't forget his requests in the future."	Her judge sees you as incompetent or defective and is giving you advice to fix you.
"It's important to get top-priority work done on time."	Her judge has taken a moralistic stance, evaluated your actions as "bad," and chosen to correct you.
"You think that's bad. Do you know what my old boss did to me? He told me to 'shape up or ship out' in front of the whole office!"	Her judge is egotistically attempting to shift attention to herself. Her commiseration perpetuates her judge's cynical world view. Dr. Eric Berne, in his book, *Games People Play*, referred to commiseration as playing the game of "Ain't it Awful."
"Didn't you understand the importance of what he wanted? How could you forget it? Have you done things like this before? Why didn't you stay late and finish it?"	The judge is questioning you to expose what is wrong with your thinking and your behavior.
"I can see why he'd be upset. Managers need to be able to count on employees to carry out their requests."	The judge is taking the superego or parent position, projecting it onto your boss and siding with him.

Table 5 – Summary of Judge Listening Techniques

JOAN'S WORDS	HER JUDGE'S THINKING
"You're really bringing this up to make a statement about the company's leadership."	Joan's judge has judged your motivation to be "bad" and thinks you are keeping it from yourself. She is telling you what your real motivation is.
"You're upset because you see your boss as another victimizer. When you were a child you saw yourself as a victim of your father's anger and now your manager is reminding you of your father. That's why you're so afraid of him."	Her judge is judging you negatively and hiding her judgment behind the mask of a psychological explanation.

In each of these attempts Joan was trying to help you. Unfortunately, her judge took over. She didn't know how to listen effectively and therefore probably didn't help you feel better. Some of her attempts may have left you feeling worse. Your hope for being understood was not met.

Now let's imagine that Joan listens consciously to you. The dialog would sound like this.

Listening with True Empathy

Joan: "Boy, that sounds like a rough experience."

You: "Yeah, it was."

Joan: "Were you upset when he spoke to you like that?"

You: "I was really embarrassed when he said that in front of the others."

Joan: "Would you rather have been spoken to more respectfully?"

You: "Yes, or at least in private."

Did you find being listened to in this way more emotionally satisfying? Would it encourage you to share more?

Truly empathic listening focuses on what the speaker is saying, as the story unfolds. It goes directly to the heart of the problem by

- validating the speaker's energy imbalance, their feeling;
- identifying the unmet hope;
- meeting the unmet hope, in whole or in part, by understanding it.

By connecting with your hope, Joan let you feel worthy of respect, even if you had made a mistake. In this way, conscious listening is unlike other listening models.

To summarize what we have learned so far, see Table 6.

Alarm and Self-awareness: We notice the first inkling of an upset feeling inside us, which tells us that the judge has reacted fearfully to some stimulus. Fear is essential in the judge's dynamics and, although its causes may be unconscious, the signs of our emotion are always available to conscious awareness. We become aware of our muscle tension or angry thoughts. Becoming aware of our emotions is the key to becoming conscious.

Center: We remember that the cause of our anger or fear resides in the judge's misperception of the other person. Our judge has seen their judge, not who they are or what they really want. Our judge generated our upset feeling. We breathe and remember that we are OK, that we can choose to think rationally. We don't have to react without thinking. We can choose how to respond by practicing self-restraint. In the space between the stimulus and response we become conscious and find freedom from the judge. We become willing to see things differently.

Choose to understand the other person by looking for the positive intention in them. They are trying to get their hopes met. Because they are imperfect and encumbered by the judge, they often do this clumsily, but their action or communication is really a call for help, which we mistakenly perceived as an attack. Our upset is the result of choosing the defend goal. We choose a new goal—to connect.

So, we reach out to the other person. We do this in such a way as to let them know that:

- We are eager to hear them and do not assume to understand beforehand.

- We are not judging them.

- We are charitable and only want to see and know their positive hope.

- We have complete trust that their conscious self will hear us and answer.

Listen: Listening with true empathy has two elements: guessing at the other person's feelings and guessing at their hopes.

Table 6 – **Listening with True Empathy**

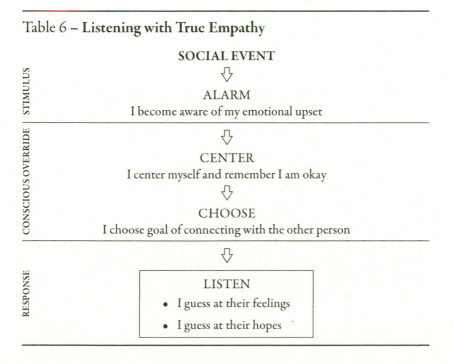

	SOCIAL EVENT
STIMULUS	⇩
	ALARM
	I become aware of my emotional upset
CONSCIOUS OVERRIDE	⇩
	CENTER
	I center myself and remember I am okay
	⇩
	CHOOSE
	I choose goal of connecting with the other person
RESPONSE	⇩
	LISTEN
	• I guess at their feelings
	• I guess at their hopes

Guess at their feelings

In a conflict situation, the other person's well-being has been thrown off balance by fear. We compassionately validate their experience by helping them describe it. We don't know exactly what another person is feeling behind their words, so we guess.

The following examples are statements made by people in pain, followed by various guesses (italicized) we could make at the feeling behind the words.

"My boss yelled at me to 'shape up or ship out!'"

> *Did you feel hurt?*
>
> *Did you feel embarrassed?*

"Darn, I just can't quite get this right!"

> *Are you frustrated?*
>
> *Are you feeling annoyed?*

"You didn't call all week."

> *Were you worried?*
>
> *Were you angry?*

"First they tell me to do it one way, then they tell me to do it another way."

> *Do you feel confused?*
>
> *Do you feel frustrated?*

By guessing, we let the person in pain know that we are genuinely interested in how they feel. We don't expect to be exactly correct in our guess. Our guess, however, alerts their conscious mind to what we are seeking to understand and, because they want to be understood, they tell us their feeling. Mutually identifying the nature of their feeling aids understanding and restores their balance.

Guess at their hopes

We show our desire to understand their unmet intention, their call for help. Their hope is their real motivation and is always positive. Because we don't know what it is, we expect to be a little off target in our guess. Our charitable guess shows our acceptance of them as good, which disarms their judge.

Here are various statements made by a person who is upset, followed by guesses we could make at their possible unmet hope:

"He's mean!"

Were you hoping to be treated kindly?

"They are so strict with rules around here."

Would you like freedom to be creative?

"It ticks me off when they make us stay late."

Were you hoping to have your time respected?

"Julian just wouldn't stop talking last night."

Would you like to have been heard?

Would you have preferred quiet?

"You just don't seem to care about what I want."

Would you like attention?

Would you like to be heard?

These guesses may seem self-evident, but to the person who is upset and trying to be understood, they are very welcome. Mutually identifying the nature of their feeling helps understanding and restores their balance.

Often guessing at someone's hope requires creative thinking. We need to put ourselves in their place and try to imagine *what could they be hoping?* Developing this willingness to find a positive intention where one may not be readily apparent takes practice. In the beginning it is helpful to refer to the list of hopes in the previous chapter.

Imagine you are working on a project with your father. You see what appears to be a better way to get the job done and you start in, at which point he says:

"You think you can do any damn thing you please."

And you reply, *"Do you think your way of doing it is better?"* or *"Would you like things to be done in a predictable way?"*

Notice how, by using these hope guesses, you didn't take what he said personally. If you defended yourself and said, "No, I don't," you would have shown that you believed his intention was to attack; you would have validated the attack by defending against it. This would make him appear "bad" in your eyes and lock him into judge consciousness.

By guessing at his possible hopes for agreement or predictability, you avoided this. Your guesses bypassed his judge and required him to consciously examine his hopes to see if you guessed accurately. In the process of examining his hopes, he will discover it and verbalize it to set the record straight. He might reply something like "No, I just think we'd get done faster if you did it the way I asked you." *Voilà*, his hope.

Listening with true empathy, we don't hear attack because we know it is not the speaker's real motivation. We know that his expression, however awkward, is a call for help, a desire to be heard and known.

We have now learned the two basic guesses that allow us to listen consciously. Let's see how they might sound in an everyday conflict situation. First we'll see how Esther, an employee at a retail clothing store, might unconsciously respond to a customer returning a dress. You may notice the judge lurking in Esther's language.

Typical Listening Example (judge in charge)

A middle-aged woman entered the store, threw a dress on the counter and said, "This store claims to sell high quality clothing. When I washed this dress the colors ran. It's ruined. I want my money back."

Esther smiled and replied, "All our materials have been tested for color-fastness. See, it says so on the label. Did you follow the instructions? Was the water too hot? What kind of detergent did you use?"

"Hey wait a minute. Are you saying this is my fault?"

"No. I'm just trying to figure out how this could have happened. We've sold a lot of these dresses and this has never happened before."

"Look, I don't want to debate this with you. All I want is my money back. Are you going to give it to me or not?"

"Yes, of course. Would you like to make an exchange? We just received these new dresses over here..."

"No! I don't want to be hassled. I want to return the dress. Please refund my money, now!"

Now let's play it again.

Example of Listening with True Empathy

"This store claims to sell high quality clothing," the customer said. "When I washed this dress the colors ran. It's ruined. I want my money back."

Esther paused and replied, "Of course, I'll process the refund right now. It must have been upsetting [feeling guess] to have the colors run in the wash. Were you planning to wear it for a special occasion?" [hope guess]

"Yes, I'm giving a presentation at a conference on Friday."

"So you really want to look professional." [hope guess]

"Yes, now I don't know what I'll do."

"Well, we just received these new dresses, which I think look very professional. Perhaps one of them would work for Friday. If not, I know two stores in the mall you can try."

"I'll take a look. Thanks for your help."

This time, when Esther noticed her initial resentment toward the customer, she practiced conscious override. Instead of defense, she chose to accept what the customer said and to hear her call for help. She focused on actively listening to the customer's feeling and her hope, "to look professional."

The Goal of Effective Listening

Our goal in conscious communication is not to change the other person, nor to get them to meet our hopes at the expense of their own. Our goal is to establish connection. When we communicate with honesty, vulnerability, and true empathy, we become aware of the goodness in them. This heals and brings about mutual agreement.

Most people don't know how to do this. When they feel afraid they retreat from their hearts into their heads where their judges relentlessly search for reasons to blame.

Attack language and violence occur when people are afraid and don't know how to express themselves. Trapped in their heads, they project fear onto others, where they feel threatened by it and want to get rid of it. They attack, first in thought and then with violent words or actions.

Their judgments and attacks are tragically misguided attempts to meet their hopes. With conscious listening, we shift their attention from their heads to their hearts. Let's look at an example:

Alex came into my teenage boys' group and sat down noisily.

"You know this program really sucks," he said. "I only come here for the food."

"Hi Alex," I responded, "Is something going on that you're upset about?"

"No."

"Well, would you be willing to check in first today? Anything happen last week?"

"Nothing major. My parents told me they're getting divorced."

Alex was in pain. When people are in pain they seem to be attacking. When we replay videotaped scenes of people in pain talking, we can point out the attack language. But if we pay attention with our hearts, it's clear that these people really want loving attention.

Someone's call for help, even if it sounds nasty, is a call to for us to listen. Let's follow Alex a little further.

A few months later, after his mother had moved to Michigan, Alex said:

"My father's new girlfriend brought her son over to my house. What a little jerk that kid is. He said he wanted me to be his older brother and I beat the crap out of him."

"It sounds like he wants to be your friend. Did you really hit him?"

"I almost broke his nose; it was all swollen. My father was furious with me."

I was shocked. But experience told me that if I judged Alex's behavior he wouldn't come back. We'd lose our connection, which was one of the only things helping him to deal with his parents' divorce.

"It sounds like you were really angry."

"My dad's such a jerk."

"Are you upset because you wish your mother was still around?"

"Yeah."

"Would you like to be living with her?"
"Yes."

He looked down to prevent anyone from seeing tears in his eyes. Alex's sadness needed to come out and to be shared in order for him to heal his loss. This wasn't psychotherapy. It was simply listening to his pain.

Later Alex and I were able to talk about how hitting the other boy was a mistake. He knew that. He had been overwhelmed at losing his mother and full of anger at his dad's girlfriend, whom he saw as responsible for the divorce. But when he admitted his violence to me, he was taking a risk to trust me. He wasn't ready to have me judge and criticize him.

People in pain do not welcome our telling them that they are wrong and need to be fixed. They want compassion and understanding. When they get advice instead, they often become angry.

When we listen consciously we don't give advice. We listen. Only after the other person has been fully heard do they return to center. It doesn't take long, and then they are able to hear us.

Listening with true empathy, we help others think in terms of what they want for themselves rather than what they "should" do. Alex also loved his father; he wanted love and understanding, not to hurt someone. But his judge limited his options and sparked anger in him. After he had been heard by me, Alex settled down and came up with some nonviolent ways to communicate with his family.

Connecting Feeling to Hope

When we are in a conflict with another person, empathizing with their feelings only begins to center them. They are still unaware that their unmet hope is the cause of their pain, and they mistakenly blame the cause of their feeling on us. So we guess in a way that suggests the connection between their feeling and their hope. This helps them to understand what is going on inside them.

Thus, if someone says, "You're ungrateful," we might guess, "Are you annoyed because you'd like to have your contribution appreciated?"

Linking the feeling, "annoyed," to the hope, "appreciation," with the words *because you* helps the other person to understand the logical connection between their unmet hope and their resulting feeling. Demonstrating empathy for both the feeling and the hope that caused it is true empathy.

When people are upset, usually all they can think of is what they don't want. So we listen for what is behind what they don't want, and help them get clear on what they do want. To do this *we always rephrase their hope in positive language.*

Imagine a man saying, "I can't stand that school bus driver. She hogs the road and stops every three houses. I was late for work this morning."

If we say, "Sounds like you're angry at her," we would acknowledge the man's feeling but miss the hope. The danger is in connecting with his judge rather than with his conscious self, perpetuating his attacking frame of mind.

Focusing on what a person doesn't want lends itself to negative solutions. The easiest way to take care of something we don't want is to eliminate it. For example, shooting the bus driver would eliminate her as a driving problem. Thinking in terms of what we don't want is the root cause of violence.

So instead we could positively rephrase the man's statement with a positive focus, "Are you frustrated because you want to get to work on time?" Oriented toward meeting the person's hope, this phrase encourages other solutions to emerge, such as leaving at a different time or taking a different route.

We don't know what is going on inside another person and no two situations are the same. Each calls for a creative response. Words or formulas may be useful learning devices but our shift in attitude is what is important.

The Jewish philosopher Martin Buber described the attitude for this kind of listening: "Each person has a sacred uniqueness, which requires of us a reaction which can not be prepared beforehand. It demands nothing of what is past. It demands presence, responsibility. It demands us." We set aside our own agendas and give our full attention.

Our listening requires taking an active role, particularly if the other person is talking without a pause. To help the other person and to truly show our interest, *we interrupt them* to guess at their feeling and hope. Surprisingly, they do not see our guess as an interruption. On the contrary, their conscious self welcomes this sign of our desire to understand at a deeper level.

We continue to listen consciously until the other person is fully heard. As one feeling and hope is revealed, connected with and resolved, the one underneath reveals itself. The process is like peeling the proverbial onion: we move to deeper emotional layers. When people have been fully heard they stop talking, relax, appear lighter and may even give us a definitive "yes." Because consciousness is required on both sides for a hope to be met, returning them to conscious center is the only way we can get our hopes met.

The Value of Conscious Listening

Connection is the greatest gift we can provide another person. The Buddhist teacher, Thich Nhat Hanh, said, "Understanding a person brings us the power to love and accept him." By connecting with the life and love in someone else, we call forth their goodness and our own. They then think more clearly and have access to their full range of inner resources, allowing them to creatively resolve conflict and make healthy choices.

When a listener is patient and unconditionally loving, miraculous changes can occur. This has been repeatedly demonstrated in the Attitudinal Healing work of Dr. Gerald Jampolsky. Jampolsky describes how a boy of twelve who had suffered brain damage made an astounding recovery as a result of being listened to by a group of his peers. His conclusion: "The kids demonstrated that love is really listening."

Conscious listening does not require that we like or agree with what another person is saying, nor that we will do what they request. Our respect for them is revealed by our being fully present, focusing our attention on the message they are expressing in the moment. This requires clearing our consciousness of whatever preconceived ideas or judgments we may have been harboring. It requires letting go our grievances and defensiveness.

Additional Listening Skills

There are three supplemental listening skills: prompting, paraphrasing and centering, which we can use to sustain a high quality connection with others.

Prompting: We prompt to show our desire to hear more. Prompts tell the other person we would like them to continue to give us information. Non-verbal prompts include: smiles, head nods, eye contact or leaning slightly forward. Verbal prompts are phrases such as "Then what?," "Tell me more," and "That's interesting." They are ways of letting the other person know we are paying attention. Short sounds such as "unh hunh" and "umm" are also supportive and encouraging.

Paraphrasing: We paraphrase to verify our understanding of the content of what they are saying and move the communication along.

Putting the other person's idea into our own words gives them feedback about how we are interpreting their message. It gives them the opportunity to confirm that what we heard is what they meant. It also gives them the opportunity to explain their idea more thoroughly if they need to. Or, when the speaker hears our paraphrase, they may decide they would rather say something else. This is helpful because it gets them deeper into what they want to say.

When we begin our paraphrase, it is useful to take ownership for a possible misinterpretation. Some helpful ownership phrases are: "What I hear you saying is... ," "It sounds like you... ," "Do you mean...," "In other words... ," "Are you saying... ." It is easier for the other person to admit to a miscommunication if we indicate that we may have heard it incorrectly.

Paraphrasing is a handy tool, but we don't want to overdo it. Not every group of statements needs to be paraphrased. We use this technique when:

- We really do not understand and need to clarify.

- The message is so important that we feel the need to confirm our understanding.

- We want the other person to feel that we are trying hard to understand their viewpoint.

- We need to bring the conversation to a close in a respectful way.

After listening to someone, we should be careful not to destroy the connection we have made by immediately disagreeing. Understanding someone doesn't mean we necessarily agree with them. We may disagree strongly, but we are cautious at this point. We respect the other person's right to his point of view and feelings. We can add our point of view without denigrating theirs.

Centering

Centering ourselves is a key skill in its own right. If we tune in to what's going on inside us we can become aware of and accept how we feel. This gives us perspective on ourselves, which is in itself calming. We can then intuitively sense the appropriate thing to do in the moment. For example, we may very much want to help another person who is suffering, yet be afraid of their suffering and embarrassed that we are afraid of it. By centering we can honor our own internal state. An excellent example of this is offered in the book, *How Can I Help?* Here the author, after describing his personal discomfort while visiting a sick person, talks about the value of admitting it to himself.

> To acknowledge our humanness, with its mixture of empathy and fear, strengthens our helping hand... Our fear is awakened not just by the suffering but by the intensity of our heart's reaction to it. The ego [judge] may have been frightened into all kinds of defense mechanisms to control our innate generosity. But mercy and kindness are our first impulses. Natural compassion was our starting point.

So we tune in to our calm center and consciously listen to ourselves. Acknowledging and admitting our discomfort in the presence of suffering allows us to be present for the other person.

Now we can begin, perhaps for the first time, to hear them. Less busy pushing away suffering, less frenzied having to do something about it, we're able to get a sense of what *they're* feeling, of what *they* feel they need. We may be startled to discover that what they've been asking for all along is entirely different from what we've been so busy offering: "All I want is for you to sit down here next to me."

Repeating a phrase such as "Let peace extend from my mind to yours" to ourselves can help us maintain our conscious intention to be helpful.

Alternatives to Listening

There are times when listening is not appropriate. Here are two alternate, non-attacking responses:

Laughing: We laugh to show no harm was done and to center the other person. This works well for instances in which our judge may feel insulted, but we can let it go. Or it may be a situation in which more in-depth discussion is either not needed or would tend to make a mountain out of a molehill. Sensitivity to other people is important so they don't think we are laughing at them.

Leaving: If we are overwhelmed and need to get help to center ourselves, we can leave.

When we are in a lot of pain we may need a break from the confrontation until we can get centered. We may need to talk with a friend who can support us by listening to us in an accepting way. This restores our emotional balance so we can return and communicate effectively in the charged situation. People in pain who can't get that kind of support can become verbally or physically violent. A dangerous situation is an excellent reason to leave.

Conscious Listening Is Radically New

Conscious listening produces a double shift in consciousness that changes our lives. The first occurs in us when we shift from negative judgment to conscious override and guess at another person's goodness. At this point we are riding on faith—that the other person is motivated by a hope—even though our eyes and ears are giving us evidence to the contrary. When the other person hears our guess they have to shift to conscious thought and, almost before they know it, they share their positive hope.

What joy and satisfaction there is when this happens! For us, our trust in human goodness has been confirmed. From their perspective, two things happen. First, because of the shift in thinking required to answer our question, they now recognize themselves as good. And second, they experience us as benevolent. We have created an experience of unconditional positive regard.

This satisfaction is hard to come by using other models of communicating. Virtually all other helping and conflict resolution communication models accept the judge's perception of someone as deficient or not well intended and therefore needing to be fixed. This assumption carries a tragic flaw because the other person instantly realizes he has been negatively judged and either resists the judgment or believes it. If he resists, he is locked in the unconscious attack and defend mode. If he accepts the negative judgment, his self-esteem drops and he feels diminished or guilty, all the while resenting the person who judged him negatively.

Let's look at what is perhaps the most widely recognized model for helpful listening, developed by Robert Carkhuff. The goal is to make the person being listened to accountable for their experiences and, according to Carkhuff, there are three ways to do this: personalizing meaning, personalizing problems, and personalizing goals.

1. Personalizing Meaning: "You feel ___ because you (meaning)."

   Carkhuff uses this statement as an example, "You feel angry that your right to choose has been violated." This supports the person's negative judgment of the situation and blaming of the violator.

   A conscious listening response would be, "Are upset because you want your right to choose to be acknowledged?"

2. Personalizing Problems: "You feel ___ because you cannot (problem)."

   In response to a person who is in distress because he or she has been unable to find a job, Carkhuff's listening response is: "You feel hopeless because you cannot manage to get a job." This supports a negative view of self.

   A conscious listening response would be "Are you unhappy because you would like to have a job?"

3. Personalizing Goals: "You feel ___ because you cannot (problem) and you want to (goal)."

   In response to a person who was disappointed over some unsatisfactory interactions with potential employers, Carkhuff's listening response is: "You feel disappointed because you cannot relate effectively to potential employers and you want to be able to relate effectively with them." The self-judgment, "cannot relate effectively," is not helpful.

   A conscious listening response would be: "Do you feel disappointed because you want to be able to relate effectively with potential employers?"

Carkhuff's model makes people accountable for their experiences by supporting their judge's negativity. Conscious listening makes people accountable for their experiences by supporting their positive intentions. There is a world of difference.

Models for listening have validated the judge's decisions because when they were developed we didn't know that almost all human perception and communication is unconsciously determined. They didn't know that when the judge is in charge, clear perception is impossible. The formulators of earlier models didn't realize that they were supporting unconscious negative judgments.

Table 7 – The Complete Conscious Listening Model

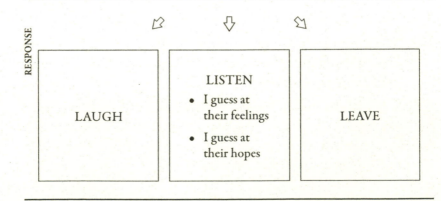

SOCIAL EVENT

⇩

STIMULUS

ALARM
I become aware of my emotional upset

⇩

CONSCIOUS OVERRIDE

CENTER
I center myself and remember I am okay

⇩

CHOOSE
I choose goal of connecting with the other person

RESPONSE

↰   ⇩   ↱

| LAUGH | LISTEN
• I guess at their feelings
• I guess at their hopes | LEAVE |

Conscious listening is truly empathic, helping both parties to connect with and to accept each other. Table 7 brings together what we have covered in this chapter.

Almost anybody can learn to think or believe or know but not a single human being can be taught to feel. Why? Because whenever you think or you believe or you know, you're a lot of other people; but the moment you feel, you're nobody-but-yourself.

– e. e. cummings

CHAPTER SIX

Conscious Speaking

Listening to and understanding another person's hopes is not complete communication. We have our own hopes, which must be understood by others if we are to experience joy and inner peace. And so we need to speak to others in a way that allows them to hear our feelings and hopes.

This is not easy. In a conflict our judge is working, but our conscious mind is not. We feel upset. The other person's judge is aware that we are upset and expects to be blamed for it. This is a set up for disaster. To avoid being seen as attacking, we must learn to speak in a new way—consciously—so the other person hears us with his or her conscious mind.

People have been trying to find a better way to speak for a long time. Thirty years ago Dr. Thomas Gordon, founder of Parent Effectiveness Training, popularized the "I-message" model. Using this model, the person speaking takes responsibility by using the word "I," as when a mother says to her child, "I hate to see my living room all dirtied up as soon as you come home from school. I feel discouraged about that after I've worked hard to clean it up." An I-message is less attacking than blaming the other person with a "you-message," such as, "You're messy and don't appreciate a clean house."

A generation has grown up using I-messages. Unfortunately, even with "I-messages," our judges manage to run the conversation. Let's see how.

Your Judge Is Attacking Your Friends

When I asked the members of a communication class for examples of when they had a loving intention but were misunderstood, Amanda told this story.

She and her husband, David, were at home on their first weekend in three months. Both had been working long hours at their jobs and Amanda was looking forward to relaxing together. On Saturday morning she was sitting on the couch, reading *Harper's*. She heard David's footsteps and hoped he would sit down next to her, put his arm around her and say something loving. David, however, walked right past her into the garage and began working on his car. Amanda was deeply disappointed.

Amanda decided to express how she felt using an I-message. A few minutes later when David came back into the room, Amanda looked up and said to him:

"I feel hurt when you ignore me. Why don't you talk to me?"

"Oh for crying out loud!" David replied. "I spend 10 minutes on the car and I get grief for it. Why are you always on my case?"

Amanda was shocked and confused. "What? Me on your case? Why on earth are you so touchy this morning?"

"Touchy! There you go. You want to see touchy? I've had it! I need car parts. See you later." And off he went.

The class's sympathies rushed to Amanda. Here she was, trying to connect with David, using an I-message, and he blew up at her. The class wondered what kind of person David must be to respond to her so harshly. They saw him as self-centered, defensive and unloving.

What was really going on? Was there anything Amanda could do about it?

The class thought the problem was worth a full examination. During the following week Amanda asked David about what he had been thinking when he got mad at her. He said he was thinking, *You're making me into the bad guy.* At our next class we considered his point of view in light of the words Amanda had spoken. Listed below are the class's guesses as to what David's specific thoughts might have been in response to Amanda's words.

Amanda's words	David's thoughts:
"I feel hurt when you"	*She's saying I hurt her. I didn't. I just walked by.*
"ignore me."	*She's decided my intention was to ignore her. It wasn't.*
"Why don't you"	*This doesn't feel good.*
"talk to me?"	*She's implying I never talk to her. That's not true. Why didn't she talk to me?*

Looking at David's thoughts on the flipchart, the class began to see how David heard Amanda's words as attacking. I suggested that

Amanda's question, "Why don't you talk to me?" didn't feel good to David because people often use "why" questions to expose what is wrong with someone else's thinking. I then asked the class to imagine what possible attack thoughts Amanda's judge could have had about David:

Possible Attack Thoughts of Amanda's Judge	Type of Attack
David was wrong to hurt me by ignoring me.	Blame
David must be a bad, or defective (stupid) person to do this.	Negative label
Because David hurt me, he should feel bad about it (implied).	Inducing guilt
David should admit he was wrong, apologize and fix it (implied).	Coercion

Amanda admitted that, unconsciously at least, she may well have had these kinds of thoughts. Her use of an I-message didn't conceal her underlying thoughts from David's judge. All of her judgments were instantly perceived by David's judge. His automatic reaction was to attack.

Was David unloving? As part of her follow-up, Amanda also asked David what had been going on in his head before their fight, when he first saw her reading. He said he had been thinking *Amanda looks so content on the couch. She has been so busy she hasn't had a chance to read her magazine. I'll respect her private time, fix the tape player in my car and we can go for a ride later.* His caring thoughts came as a surprise to Amanda. She felt embarrassed for judging him wrongly.

But when he walked by she *had* been disappointed. What could she do? Deny her disappointment? Certainly not. Trying to bottle up feelings is unhealthy. Amanda needed to rephrase her feeling so she was not attacking and, in doing so, tell the more vulnerable truth.

As a class we studied the conscious speaking skills that follow in this chapter, and Amanda thought how she could have applied them in her situation. Then we role-played the scene again, from the point where Amanda was reading her magazine on the couch. Here is what happened:

The man who was role-playing David walked right by her. As his back receded, Amanda felt angry. This time she noticed that her first thought was *Damn him and that car; that's all he cares about.* She saw her anger as an alarm to become conscious. She decided to center herself and remembered her hope for connection. Then she went up to the man role-playing David and said, "David, I have an idea how we can get along better. Do you have a minute?"

"Yeah, what is it?"

"When you walked by without speaking to me, I felt sad because

Table 9 – **Example of Conscious Speaking**

AMANDA'S WORDS	ELEMENT OF CONSCIOUS SPEAKING
"David, I have an idea how we can get along better. Do you have a minute?"	This opener told him her initial hope and asked whether he was ready to talk.
"When you walked by without speaking to me"	This was the fact of what he had done, with no judgment of him.
"I felt sad"	She expressed her feeling.
"because I"	She took responsibility for generating her feeling. She didn't blame him for it.
"was hoping to spend some time with you."	She took responsibility for generating her feeling. She didn't blame him for it.
"Would you be willing to sit down and talk with me sometime soon?"	She made a connecting request.

I was hoping to spend some time with you. Would you be willing to sit down and talk with me sometime soon?"

"Sure," the man playing David warmly replied.

Everyone in the room experienced his response as genuine. Amanda was pleased because this time her use of conscious speaking had allowed her to say what she was hoping without triggering David's judge.

Amanda's communication provides an excellent example of the elements of conscious speaking. See Table 8.

These elements combine to make a whole conscious speaking statement. In Table 9 each element is presented with the purpose it serves.

Let's look at how the parts of conscious speaking work. Each element is presented with a suggested format showing a simple way for you to apply the idea.

The Opener

Example:
"David,   I have an idea how we can get along better. Do you have a minute?"

Format:
Person's name   +our hope for the conversation

+ respectful request to talk

In a potential conflict, situation people's defenses are easily triggered. If their defensive emotions kick in they are no longer able to hear us. So how we begin our communication is of the utmost importance. The purpose of the opener is to gain the attention of the other person's conscious mind without triggering a defensive, negative judgment from their judge. In the opener we share our hope for the communication—a positive outcome such as mutual understanding or a better relationship.

A good opener meets two criteria; it sets a positive purpose for the conversation and it is respectful of the other person. For example, Harriet, the manager of a kitchenware store, received a complaint from a customer about how a salesperson, Janet, had treated her. Harriet wanted to discuss the complaint with Janet and wanted Janet to be open to changing her behavior in the future. Harriet began this way:

"Hi Janet, I want your help in finding a way to resolve a customer satisfaction problem. Do you have a minute to talk about it now?"

We can also use an opener to let someone know the kind of response we're hoping for. Martha was hesitant to talk with her husband, Daryl, about a conflict at home because Daryl never seemed to listen to her. He always immediately started to talk about his own point of view. Here is the opener Martha used with Daryl:

Table 9 – Conscious Speaking Elements

ELEMENT	PURPOSE
Opener	The opener sets a positive tone by expressing our initial hope for the conversation and respectfully asks if the other person would like to talk now.
Fact	The fact lets the other person know, without any judgment on our part, what happened that affected our well-being and caused us to want to speak.
Feeling	Our feeling statement exposes our heart by letting the other person know the emotion we are experiencing in relation to what happened.
Hope	Our hope statement shows them we are not blaming them, but rather asking for their help.
Request	The request provides the other person with an immediate way show they would like to help us.

"Daryl, I'm feeling annoyed at what's been happening. I'd like to tell you what I've been thinking and feeling and then, when I'm finished, have you tell me what you heard me say. I want to know that you've heard me. Would you be willing to do this?"

In addition to meeting the two criteria for a good opener, Martha let Daryl know how she would like to be listened to and the nature of the response she would like to receive.

Here is another example of an opener Martha came up with for a touchy subject with Daryl:

"Daryl, I'd like to find a way we can both feel comfortable about how our family income is spent. Would this be a good time to talk about it?"

If we discover that the other person is not ready to listen to us, we rely on our intuition to tell us whether this is because they are emotionally off-center and first need to be heard by us, or whether they are just otherwise busy and we need to arrange another time to talk.

The opener serves the vital function of setting the tone. We can't make a good opener until we have consciously overridden our attack thoughts and set a new goal.

Once we have opened the conversation, particularly when we are upset, we need to let the other person know what we are upset about.

The Fact

Example:
"When   you walked past me without speaking"

Format:
"When"   + the action, words or thought that
                triggered you.

Stating a simple fact when we are in a conflict situation is a challenge. Our judge has already reacted unconsciously, putting the other person in a negative light. Fortunately, we can notice our upset feelings and use our awareness as an alarm to wake up. We pause and in this calm moment, override our judge. Then we state the event or thought that triggered us without analyzing, evaluating, or judging the other person. We restrict ourselves to the bare facts of the matter.

The first statement in each of the following pairs is judgmental, with the judgmental words italicized. The second is a factual restatement.

"You were in a bad *mood* yesterday."	Judgmental
"Yesterday I heard you say, 'I'm fed up with all this stuff.'"	Factual
"You are really *pushy* when it comes to your marketing plan."	Judgmental
"You asked me to put my work aside and help with your marketing plan."	Factual
"You *often forget* things I ask you to do."	Judgmental
"You didn't put the trash out twice last month."	Factual

A fact contains no evaluation, judgment or interpretation of the other person's motives. Evaluation and judgment only produce resentment in the other person, who then becomes defensive and unlikely to hear the important part of our message.

Here are two more examples:

"When you *criticized* me..."	Judgmental
"When you said you didn't like the way I did that..."	Factual

"When you expect me to clean up your dishes..."	Judgmental
"When I saw dirty dishes on the counter..."	Factual

To forgo being "right" about how the other person is wrong requires conscious self-restraint. Here is an enlightening exercise for you to try:

Think of something someone did or said that you didn't like. Then write it down in a factual statement. To distinguish objective fact from judgment in this situation, it might be helpful to think of what actions or words a video camera would have recorded. Keep your statement brief. If what they did has happened more than once, don't generalize. Just mention the last time or two about which you can be specific.

Look at your fact statement. Would the other person agree with what you've written? If not, pare it down until you are sure they would. This is your fact. It may seem disappointingly weak. That is OK. The point is only to let the other person know what you are talking about. If you want to connect with them and get your hope met, you must forgo the pleasure of being "right" about them.

Caution: To preserve another person's hope to be fully understood for who they are, we need to be particularly careful about using the verb "to be" in its various forms: "is, was, are, were," etc. When applied to people, it is so all-encompassing that it distorts the facts. For instance, if we say "Carl is lazy," nothing after the verb "is" limits Carl's laziness in any way. So anyone hearing us could think:

- Carl exhibits only lazy behavior.
- Carl will be lazy in all situations and at all times.

We have joined Carl with lazy in such a way that we can't separate the two. Saying to someone "you are this" or "you are that" negative quality is not only inaccurate, but it attacks their identity as a good person. Facts, such as, "Carl didn't follow up on my request last Thursday," are more accurate and non-attacking.

Feelings

We all know how our bodies change when we feel certain emotions. When we are afraid our hearts beat faster and our skin cools. Each feeling state provides a distinctive bodily readiness to act. Anger gives us the strength to fight. Sadness gives us the softness to grieve.

Our perception of what is happening to us provokes our feelings. When we perceive a threat to our well-being, we feel fear. When we perceive benevolence, we feel whole and happy. What we hadn't realized until now, is that our unconscious judgment determines our perception.

There are two basic emotional states, fear and love. Within each of these are a variety of subsidiary emotions. Depending on how we think about a situation, our judge transforms fear into one of its secondary emotions: sadness, guilt or anger. Here is how our thinking generates each of these emotions:

If we determine that our hope is lost or unattainable then we feel some form of *sadness*, such as grief or despair. In this case we are convinced that we can't get our hopes met.

If we think that there is something wrong with ourselves, we blame ourselves and we feel *guilt*. Guilt is sadness or anger directed at ourselves in reaction to the thought that we have done something "wrong" or are defective. Our judge doesn't like to feel too much of the inner tension that comes with guilt and frequently blames other people so he can think of himself as victimized instead.

When we think that someone has intentionally come between us and the fulfillment of our hope we feel *angry*. Our blame of the other person is the unconscious projection of our judge's own guilt and fear. We see the other person as having done us a "wrong," which we can "right" by punishing them or by seizing what we want. When angry, we want to make the other person feel guilty. Making sure that we see the other person as guilty is the judge's signature mental trick. Anger mobilizes our bodies to attack and is so powerful it can temporarily "highjack" our thought process, making it more difficult to consciously override.

Intellectually, we may know that our perception of threat is merely the projection of our judge's fearful state onto someone. But we're still upset. And we need to express our emotions. Our fear-based emotions are our calls to return to a state of well-being. Emotions need to move. The word emotion comes from Latin roots, which mean "to move out." Sharing our feelings with another person moves this energy out of ourselves. When we share our feelings with someone and experience the healing power of empathic understanding our well-being begins to be restored.

So when we are upset, we state our emotion using a feeling word such as annoyed, anxious, confused, depressed, discouraged, embarrassed, frustrated, or worried. If our hopes are being met, we use a feeling word such as: cheerful, confident, elated, glad, grateful, happy, inspired, or peaceful.

Table 10 shows the essential relationships between thoughts and feelings.

Stating Our Feelings: Sharing a feeling touches another person's heart. Stating our fear is a gift because it shows our desire to connect. We are trusting a person by letting them know how upset we are about the discrepancy between what we see happening and what we wish for. The other person's heart is drawn to respond compassionately.

There is great power in using feeling words. They speak from the heart to the heart. If people hear we are experiencing an upset emotion (and don't feel attacked), they are "hard wired" to help us return to emotional balance. As human beings, one of our profoundest hopes is to be helpful to people in need. Honest feeling statements touch our innate generosity.

Table 10 – **Using Emotions Intelligently**

FEARFUL FEELINGS / LOVE FEELING	THINKING THAT GENERATED THE FEELING	JUDGE'S USE OF THE FEELING	CONSCIOUS THINKING TO SHIFT FEELING	POSITIVE USE OF FEELING	RESULT OF "BOTTLING UP" THE FEELING
FEAR	I'm weak and I see a threat	Withdrawal, self-sacrifice; or shift to blame and anger	What am I hoping? What are they hoping?	Share feelings and hopes to connect	Anxiety, phobias, panics, obsessions
SADNESS	I'm losing or have lost something	Self-pity, try to ignore it, or shift to blame and anger	What am I hoping?	Cry, share, connect	Self-pity, shame, sickness
ANGER	You are hurting or wronging me	Attack other person and make them feel guilty	What is my unmet hope? What is their unmet hope?	Stop, acknowledge, sadness, connect, and resolve conflict	Depression, bitterness, hatred, violence
GUILT	I hurt or wronged you	Blame self, attack self	I'm sad their hope wasn't met. If I knew then what I know now, I'd have acted differently	Acknowledge sadness, connect by guessing feeling and hope	Resentment, depression, low self-esteem
HAPPINESS	My hopes are met	Becoming possessive, conditional love (I love you if...)	My hopes are met and will continue to be met	Giving, sharing, laughing, feeling happy, communicating	No fun, isolation, depression, cynicism

"I'm sad that you are leaving."

"I'm pleased that you are helping out."

"I feel frightened about my financial situation."

Feeling statements such as these catch our attention; they draw us in.

Three Cautions about Feeling Words: Not infrequently, however, under our judge's influence, we use words that sound like feeling words but are not feeling words. Although they appear to be feeling words, they attack another person.

A primary offender is the use of the phrase "I feel," followed by something that is not an emotion but some form of judgment. Look at these phrases:

"I feel that..."	What is coming next is not a feeling, but a thought.
"I feel he..."	A judgment or interpretation of another person is coming next.
"I feel you..."	A judgment of you is coming.
"I feel as if you..."	A judgment of you is coming.
"I feel like..."	A thought, not an emotion is coming.
"I feel like you..."	A judgment of you is coming.

A second misuse of feeling language by our judge is to blame other people for causing our feelings. Our blame not only implies that we know their motivation but also, by attributing negative intention to them, accuses them of being bad.

Even some of the best books on emotions fall into this trap. In the best-seller, *Emotional Intelligence*, the following statement, made by a wife to her husband, is used as an example of an emotionally intelligent communication. "When you forgot to pick up my clothes at the cleaner's, it made me feel like you don't care about me."

Ouch! The wife has *not* expressed how she feels but has made a judgment of what is going on inside her husband. Her words, "it made me feel," indicate that her husband's behavior caused her feeling. But it was her assessment of whether or not his action (or inaction) met with her hope that generated her feeling. She is in control of her perception and her hope. Thus, accusing him of causing her feeling is unfair.

Furthermore, her next words, "feel like you don't care about me," are her interpretation of his caring, not an emotion. She has used the word "feel" only to mask her negative judgment of his caring. This judgment is an attack on his self-image as a good person. Only bad husbands don't care about their wives.

Her husband's response would probably be defensive, along the lines of "But I do care about you. I'm sorry I didn't get the clothes. I had ten thousand other things I had to do. I'll get the clothes tomorrow." He would feel annoyed about her concealed attack and resentful about being pressured by guilt into picking up the clothes. So we see that her attack language probably left him feeling less caring, the opposite of what she was hoping for.

What could she have done? Speaking consciously, she might have addressed her issues with her husband in this way:

"When you didn't pick up my clothes at the cleaner's, I felt disappointed because I wanted to have the clothes by the end of the day. Would you be willing to talk with me about who can get them and when?"

A third misuse of feeling language occurs when judgmental words are masqueraded as emotions. They are used to attribute negative intentions to other people. Because they are so easily misused, here is a list of common offenders.

Judgmental Words Used in Place of Feelings

abandoned	insulted	rejected
abused	intimidated	ripped off
attacked	invalidated	smothered
blamed	left out	stupid
betrayed	let down	threatened
cheated	manipulated	tricked
controlled	misunderstood	unheard
distrusted	neglected	unwanted
dumped on	overpowered	used
hassled	patronized	violated
hurt	pressured	worthless
ignored	put down	

When we say, "I feel abandoned," we are really saying, "It was your intention to abandon, me." "Abandoned" is not a feeling. We feel sad, but our judge doesn't say that. Instead he attributes the negative intention of abandoning to the other person.

Isn't it amazing how unconscious we are of the judge's machinations?! Unless we stop and wake up, we believe his assumptions about other people. Our culture fosters the negative, attacking side of feeling expression, and we have gone along with it. We have become afraid of the honest, non-attacking expression of emotion.

Transforming a disguised attack into a feeling statement is quite simple. Here are some examples of non-feeling statements with the corresponding feeling statements in Italics:

"I feel like throwing this in your face."	*I feel angry.*
"I feel pressured."	*I feel annoyed.*
"I feel you're upset with me."	*I feel anxious, afraid.*
"I feel you don't like me."	*I feel afraid, sad.*
"When you don't say 'hello,' I feel ignored."	*I feel sad or angry.*
"I feel you're misunderstanding me."	*I feel sad, frustrated.*

Many of us are reluctant to express our feelings. We may have been discouraged or punished for doing so when we were younger, and because of this, have learned to stay in our heads. We use cognitive verbs like I think, which detach us from our feelings.

People also avoid feelings by jumping into problem solving and advice giving instead of listening. Without connection at the feeling level the emotional imbalance will not be restored and the upset feelings will remain stuck, eventually becoming toxic.

We may feel vulnerable when we put down the familiar sword and shield protection of our thinking, analyzing, and evaluating in order to expose our feelings and hopes. While this does take courage, there is tremendous strength and wisdom in being truthful about feelings. Our disclosure of feeling accesses other people's compassion and generosity. Our hearts know how to do this. We have just become rusty.

Emotions energize us and guide us. Staying with our feelings and with the feelings of others, and expressing those feelings positively, leads us to conflict resolution. Expressing our feelings responsibly greatly increases the likelihood of our hopes being met.

Feelings and Responsibility—The "Because I" Clause: Let's look at it from the perspective of the person to whom we are speaking. If we tell them they did something that makes us feel badly, then they will think they did something wrong and will then feel guilty. Guilt is psychological pressure that causes people to apologize or to defend themselves. Then, even if they do what we ask, they will be acting out of guilt, not genuine concern for us. They are likely to become resentful at being coerced into doing what they would otherwise have taken joy in—helping us get our hopes met.

We can't get what we really want by applying pressure. It's like twisting someone's arm and saying, "Tell me that you love me." Our hopes must be met *out of people's own free will*, out of the natural compassion between human beings.

Some people coerce themselves around feelings. Angela believed she caused her husband's feelings. When he was angry, she thought it was her fault and tried to do things to make him feel better. She became afraid to do anything that he didn't deem OK. She gradually became a self-appointed slave to his emotions. She resented him, but it was of her own doing.

Moving to our perspective as conscious speakers, we don't want to make other people our emotional slaves. We are therefore careful to connect our feeling statement to our hope with a "because I..." clause that acknowledges our own responsibility for our own emotion.

Imagine you cut your finger slicing a bagel, got stitches at the emergency room and called your friend, Denise, when you get home. Denise was out so you left her a message on her answering machine to call you back. She never called back. You call her the next morning and say, "When you didn't return my call, I felt disappointed *because I* hurt myself and really wanted support." In this way you have accepted responsibility for generating your own disappointment by connecting it to your unmet hope, wanting support.

You caused your own disappointment. If you had never cut your finger, and instead had been home engrossed in watching a movie, you would not have been disappointed if Denise didn't call. You might have been annoyed at the interruption if she had.

Stating Our Hope

Two students in an evening communication class demonstrated how communication improves when we link our feeling to our hope. Shari and Carletta had become friends at work, enjoyed each other's company and decided to take my class together. But Carletta said that sometimes after Shari said things, she felt uncomfortable. She remembered one of Shari's statements, "Carletta, I'm upset that you always leave your charts over there." The class pointed out that Shari hadn't connect her feeling to a hope.

For practice, Shari restated her thought, "I'm upset that you leave your charts over there because I want access to the information." Carletta said she felt valued rather than criticized when Shari spoke to her this way.

We're not used to thinking about our hopes. In a given situation, we may not be aware of what hope is clamoring for attention, but we can use our feelings to track it down. To do this we stop our activity, breathe, and ask ourselves, "What hope of mine isn't being met that could cause me to feel this way? How would I prefer the situation to be?" Then we listen to our intuition about what would please us, what we really are hoping.

Let's continue our cut finger example. Imagine you wake in the morning with a bandaged hand. You're the only one home and have to take a shower while keeping your hand dry, then get dressed and make breakfast. You notice you're upset and thinking no one loves you or cares about you; *Denise isn't a good friend. I help her out all the time and she doesn't even bother to call me back when I'm in real distress.* Then you notice your thoughts, become conscious, and think, *What hope of mine isn't being met right now?* You realize that trying to make Denise feel guilty isn't your real hope. Behind your anger and sadness is the hope to be supported.

We can confirm whether we are really on the path of our hope by monitoring how we feel as we move in that direction. When our action is meeting our hope we feel more peaceful and happy; when it is not meeting our hope, we feel more upset.

Being aware of our hopes frees us to see that if a certain person doesn't want to meet our hope, there are other possibilities. We don't have to force compliance because we can get our hope met somewhere else in a non-coercive way. If we find that Denise is out of town, we can call someone else. To realize that our hopes can always be met ensures the continuance of our peaceful mental state. It gives us patience.

When voicing our hopes, it is helpful to remember that they are general and positive. Hence it is wise to *leave other people out of our hope statements* so that they are not bound to the solution. Here is an example.

Carol and Jeff had been living together for about six months. One morning Carol put her clothes in the dryer and turned it on before leaving the house. When Jeff came home in the evening he started a wash load. When it was done he took his wet clothes out and then found Carol's clothes still in the dryer. She wasn't home, so he put them in a laundry basket next to the dryer. When Carol came home late that evening, her clothes were wrinkled.

She said to Jeff, "I'm upset because I was hoping you would hang them up instead of stuffing them in the laundry basket."

"Hoping you would hang them up" is not a hope of Carol's. It is her expectation of Jeff to act in a way that she sees as good. She has identified Jeff's behavior as the cause of her upset, which makes Jeff bad. He would probably feel defensive about this.

Let's let Carol try again, this time leaving Jeff out of her hope statement:

"When I found my blouses were wrinkled, I was upset because I was hoping to have them ready to wear."

Had she said this, Jeff would be free to realize he hadn't thought about them getting wrinkled, and to regret putting them in the basket. He now has the opportunity to volunteer to hang the blouses for her next time.

Connecting another person to our upset feeling by saying, "because I was hoping you," boxes both parties in narrowly to a situation that actually has all kinds of other possibilities for solution. We are better off to leave them open.

We must likewise be careful not to use the "because I" clause to connect our feeling to a judgmental thought.

Imagine you ask Robert: "Would you have coffee with me today?"

And Robert replies: "No, I have other things I want to do."

You feel disappointed. You could respond by sharing your hope: "I feel disappointed because I would have liked some company," and Robert is unlikely to feel judged or guilty.

But if you said "I feel disappointed because I take your 'no' as a rejection," you have taken responsibility for generating your feeling by using the "because I" clause. However, you have followed it with a thought that judges Robert's intention, "I take your 'no' as a rejection." Through this interpretation you have assumed to know that Robert's motivation was to reject you. Your judge is attempting to induce guilt.

If Robert believes your interpretation of him as the type of person who would reject someone, he will feel guilty. He may think he was "wrong" to think that whatever he wanted to do, other than have coffee with you, was more important to him. He may feel bad enough to reverse himself and (reluctantly) spend time with you. Neither of you is likely to enjoy this time. There is no winning by coercing someone through guilt. It infringes on their hopes.

The two common ways our hopes are infringed upon are:

- when someone says anything that sounds to us like criticism, attack, judgment, blame, or diagnosis.

- When someone makes a demand or request that sounds like coercion such as "you should; you have to."

The first violates our identity as a good person and the second denies our freedom to choose when and how we will give.

Now we understand how to express our hopes. However, the other person still may not know how to respond. For example, when Carol said "When I found my blouses were wrinkled, I was upset because I was hoping to have them ready to wear," Jeff may not know what to do next, how to help her. He may still think her intention is to blame him for bad behavior.

Carol can help him by letting him know what action she would like him to take. "Would you be willing to hang up the blouses next time?" This gives him a simple choice, "yes" or "no."

Making Our Request

The request lets the other person know what they can do or say to help us get our hope met. This could simply involve their responding "yes" to our question. It's an easy way to connect.

To make an appropriate request, we first decide what action we would like taken. We ask ourselves, "What do I want as a first step to help me meet my hope?" We don't use vague words in the request such as "think," "feel," or "consider." We use concrete action words such as "tell," "go," or "do." Here are two clear requests:

- "Would you be willing to take the dog to board overnight at the kennel?"

- "Will you tell me one thing I can do to correct the situation?"

Nor do we use negative language, saying what we "don't" want, as in "Please stop leaving me hanging in social situations." Instead we would say, "Next time, would you be willing to introduce me to your friends before you get involved in conversation with them?"

One way to test if a request meets our criteria for clarity is to ask ourselves, "If I were the other person, would I know exactly what to do?" Here are two examples of unclear requests that have then been made more specific:

- "I want you to understand what I'm saying."

  "Will you listen to what I'm about to say and then tell me what you heard?"

- "I'd like you to be more considerate."

"Would you be willing to reset the copier after you're done?"

We make the request in question form because we only want the other person to do what we request if they are genuinely willing. The word "please" is modern shorthand for the phrase "if it pleases you." Unfortunately, the word "please" by itself is easily incorporated into a coercive demand. Many of us have forgotten the importance of accessing the other person's willingness, the only doorway to their compassion.

The Difference Between a Request and a Demand: The unconscious influence of our judges can make it hard to recognize the difference between a request and a demand. A request brings about a response motivated by a person's desire to help. A demand coerces a response motivated by fear, guilt or shame.

We can tell whether we intended a request or a demand by our reaction if the person says "no." If they say no and we empathize with their hope that takes priority over doing what we asked, then we made a request. But if we feel angry, become coercive, or attempt to induce guilt, then we made a demand. Let's look at an example of what might occur when Georgia wants some help with the yard work.

In this example, Georgia can choose to get help either by establishing a high quality connection with her husband first, and then negotiating until she finds a way to get her hope met. Or, she can motivate him with a demand and damage the relationship. See Table 11.

Pulling All the Elements Together

Let's see an example of listening and speaking used together. Here a dialysis nurse, Colleen, perceived that a difficult situation was about to become a lot worse. A male patient, who had previously shown he had a short temper, was waiting for treatment and had just looked up at the clock.

Patient:	"I need to start my treatment in 5 minutes!"	
Colleen:	"When you see that it's 5 minutes to your usual start time and the machine isn't ready,	Fact
		Feeling
	do you feel anxious,	
		Hope
	because you want to get done on time?"	
Patient:	"It drives me nuts to get here on time and then have to sit around before my treatment starts. Then I get out late and the people who pick me up are mad at me."	
		Feeling
Colleen:	So you find it really upsetting, both for yourself and those who pick you up, when you get out of here late.	
Patient:	"Yes."	
		Feeling
Colleen:	"I can see how unpleasant that is for you."	

Table 11 – Request or Demand

If Georgia states, "Please help me in the yard for an hour."
and her husband replies, "I don't have time."

Her statement was a request if she then says:	Her statement was a demand if she then says:
CONNECTION "Do you need more time to finish what you're doing?" and negotiates with him.	JUDGMENT "You're just not willing to cooperate around the house."
	OR INDUCING GUILT "If you cared about me you'd find the time."
	OR COERCION "You can help me now or buy the food and fix your own dinner."

"When I hear you ask to start your treatment in five minutes	Fact
I feel frustrated	Feeling
because I would like to start you on the machine right now; your getting out on time	Hope
is important to me, but for safety reasons I have to prepare this equipment first.	Hope
Are you willing to let me finish this and then I'll get you started?"	Request

Patient: "Oh, O.K."

Colleen showed that she shared her patient's hope and then let him know that she had her own hope, "safety," which she needed to attend to first. Presented in this way, he was glad to let her do what she had to do.

Why Speaking This Way Is So Powerful

Everybody has one hope that you can count on—to help other people get their hopes met. This generosity of spirit is hard-wired in each of us, part of being human. Think for a moment of a time when you, out of the goodness of your heart, helped someone get one of their hopes met. You might have seen a child drop a mitten in the snow and you called their attention to it. Maybe you let an elderly or pregnant person go ahead of you in the check out line. You may have done something on a grander scale, like painting your aunt's apartment.

Whatever it was, take a minute now to reflect. Whom did you help? What were their circumstances? What were yours? What did you do? How did you do it?

Now remember how you felt when you saw how your action helped them. Participants in my workshops enjoy thinking of these times. They get a warm feeling remembering when they provided a service to someone who was temporarily in need. When they tapped into the other person's hopes, the other person appreciated it, felt grateful, and maybe even reciprocated.

The essential point of this exercise is that deep down, *everybody wants to help other people get their hopes met.* You can count on it. When we offer them a chance, without coercing them, to help us meet our hope, they are likely to respond positively.

To practice your own conscious speaking, you can now complete the situation you began earlier, in which you were asked to think of something someone did that you didn't like and to write it as a fact. Practice all the conscious speaking elements on the form on the next page. You may wish to photocopy the form to use again and again.

Here is a good way for you to get feedback on your communication. Tape record your conversation with another person during a conflict situation. Play the tape back and transcribe the dialog on the left side of the page. Then write what you were thinking on the right side.

The feedback you will gain from hearing the words you use is invaluable. The first time I tried this I was shocked to hear the discrepancy between what I thought I was communicating and what I was actually saying. After examining your transcript, think of how you could restate your words using conscious communication.

None of us is perfect. One of the best ways to learn the skills of conscious speaking is to notice the times you make mistakes. Then replay in your mind how you could have rephrased things. A summary of some of our most common mistakes appears in Table 12.

SPEAKING WORKSHEET

OPENER

Name of person with whom you are in conflict

"_____"

Your hope for the conversation "I_____

_____.

Test their readiness _____

("Is this a good time?")

FACT

"When you _____

FEELING

"I felt _____ (emotion)

HOPE

"Because I _____ (was hoping, wanted)

_____" (hope)

REQUEST

"Would you be willing to _____ ?

Table 12 – Mistakes and their Effects

MISTAKE	EFFECT
1. Analysis, judgment or evaluation of other person	Violates their right to their own feelings, hopes or intentions
2. Asking "why" someone did, felt or thought something	A sign analysis is coming next, which makes people defensive
3. Not expressing your upset feelings in an attempt to avoid hurting the other person or to avoid conflict	You are stuck with your emotional energy, feel bad about yourself and begin to resent them
4. Using a non-feeling attack word, "I feel rejected"	Sneaky way to hide your judgment of their intention (to reject)
5. Using a judgment in place of a feeling "I feel that you are unfair"	Another sneaky way to hide your evaluation of them behind "I feel"
6. Connecting other person to your feeling, "I feel sad because you said that"	You are blaming them for causing your feeling
7. Connecting yourself to the other's feeling, "You feel angry because I changed my mind"	You are saying you caused their feeling. You become stuck in "emotional slavery"
8. Threatening, blaming, coercing, inducing guilt, demanding	People may appear to do what you want in the short term, but they'll resent you and you'll pay for it later
9. Not stating your hope	People may think you're blaming or judging them
10. Not making a connecting request	People don't know what you want from them. They may assume you brought it up just to make them feel bad
11. Saying what you don't want	They don't know what you do want; eliminating what you don't want may lead to a violent solution
12. Problem-solving or giving advice before connecting with feelings and hope	The person hasn't experienced connection with you; he/she is full of his/her own emotional energy, doesn't trust you and can't hear you

*The ideal of warriorship is that the warrior should be sad and tender,
and because of that, the warrior can be very brave as well.*

– CHÖGYAM TRUNGPA

CHAPTER SEVEN

True Empathy and Anger

On a spring morning in 1998, two boys watched from the woods as students filed out of the middle school in Jonesboro, Arkansas. The fire alarm the boys had pulled was still ringing. The eleven-year-old passed a rifle to his thirteen-year-old friend. They each took aim and opened fire, killing four girls and a teacher and wounding eleven other kids. Just a few months earlier, in Paducah, Kentucky, a fourteen-year-old boy had shot students in a high school prayer group, killing three girls, paralyzing one and wounding four other students. More school shootings followed.

What surprised the nation most about this wave of shootings was the age of the perpetrators, not their sex. It is common knowledge that the vast majority of violent crimes are caused by men. The boys who did the shooting showed no remorse and had no empathy for those they shot.

Why does violence like this occur and why is it men who are more prone to act violently and to attack others?

Most men learn, as I did, to bury their emotions. Growing up in an affluent suburb of Boston, I learned early that if I showed fear or sadness I was a "sissy." As I got older, betraying even a hint of those emotions branded me a "wimp." If I expressed compassion toward another male I was called a "queer."

It is hard to overestimate the effect these words have on a boy who is struggling to form his identity and to be seen as a good person. The words "sissy," "wimp," and "queer" strip him of his male identity. He has been judged "bad," loses the respect of others and, at that impressionable age, of himself.

The following story illustrates the lengths to which I was willing to go to avoid that negative judgment.

I was walking behind the school one day when I saw a "tough" kid, Bobby, throwing rocks and breaking window after window in the school. The next day the principal came into my classroom and asked if anyone knew anything about it. I raised my hand, already feeling anxious. The principal took me into the hall and asked me to confirm what he already knew, that Bobby had done it. I nodded.

Later, on the playground, Bobby came up behind me and locked me in a stranglehold with his forearm on my throat, cutting off my air. He was several years older than me. As he lifted me off my feet I struggled as hard as I could, but I couldn't break his grip. Then the world went black. When I came to I was lying on the ground.

I didn't cry. My parents had taught me not to. I was terrified, but I was also ashamed to have been so thoroughly beaten. I felt like a wimp. I didn't tell anyone what happened; I also didn't go back to the playground, avoiding all reminders of that fearful humiliation.

I would rather have been killed than been branded a wimp.

We live in the most violent society in the world. Why? Male socialization in America is based on the preparation of soldiers. A soldier's job is to kill people. For this, anger is useful. Soldiers won't kill people if they empathize with them, so they must be taught to deny their feelings. They must deny their fear of battle, the sadness of killing, their empathy with the feelings of those they wound or kill, as well as the feelings of surviving family and friends. In a society of soldiers, of judges trained for war, is it any wonder that violence is epidemic?

Because of this training, fathers inflict emotional and physical punishment on their sons. *Learning to repress fear and sadness in the face of this trauma is the distinguishing characteristic of the rite of passage from boy to man.* When boys cut out their feeling selves, their hearts, in order to become "men," their bottled up emotional energy must go somewhere. Like alcoholic beverages fermenting at home with lids too tightly sealed, the bottles eventually explode.

Men in Pain: a Special Case

It is hard to empathize with a man who is angry. We know that men in our culture have difficulty expressing their feelings, but the depth and pervasiveness of this condition is alarming. It has been estimated that eighty percent of American men suffer from mild to severe emotional numbness. As a result, according to psychotherapist Terrence Real, Ph.D., author of *I Don't Want to Talk About It: Overcoming the Legacy of Male Depression*, most men unknowingly suffer from "covert depression." Depression occurs when anger is turned toward the self. Covert depression is an insidious, subtle form of depression lacking the usual despondent symptoms.

Covert depression is invisible. Because loss of the capacity to feel is its main symptom, most men are unaware of their depressed condition. Unconscious of what is going on inside them, these men are feeling-dead, unable to connect or form intimate relationships.

Dr. Real states that such men are more prone to externalize their pain in violence and less able to empathize with their victims.

Covert depression begins in childhood. Prior to age four or five, boys are actually more sensitive than girls. From this point on, however, they are systematically traumatized. First there is passive trauma. Parents treat boys more coldly and with greater physical distance than girls. Boys are trained to separate from their mothers and to disown their nurturing and expressive qualities.

Then most boys are actively traumatized through violent disciplining. Fathers beat their unacknowledged misery into their sons. The boys swallow it, become covertly depressed, and eventually come to identify with their fathers' rage and shamelessness. The only feeling condoned in them is anger. In attempting to hide their feelings, they externalize their pain through addictions and violence. It is impossible for boys to completely avoid the violent process of male acculturation.

As men, their sense of esteem does not come from a good sense of self, for they are extremely harsh with themselves. Nor does it come from intimate relationships, because their inability to express feelings makes them incompetent. What fragile sense of esteem they have comes from their outer achievements and how much money they make.

According to Dr. Real, however, there is reason to hope. Men can find treatment to stop addictive behaviors and therapeutically release buried childhood pain. They can establish empathy for the vulnerable child they carry within them and, through this, they can learn and practice the art of connection with others. In doing so, they heal.

Not surprisingly, most men cannot do this alone. Their lifetime training won't allow them to risk showing fear, weakness or sadness. Some men attempt to find a woman to be their emotional voice, but their own feelings remain buried. Only becoming aware of their own feelings and sharing them restores them to well-being.

Conscious communication allows this to happen.

We have an opportunity to help men wake up and come alive. For them to take this risk, they must believe that we will hear their fear and sadness and validate it without implying they are wimps. Our challenge is to hear the hope behind an angry man's words. Conscious communication requires genuine courage on the part of the both the speaker and the listener. The word courage comes from the Indo-European word for heart. Courage is the strength to be in one's heart, not to retreat to the judgmental head.

So, how do we listen to men in pain?

Listening to Anger – Giving True Empathy

Understanding what is going on psychologically can help us to overcome our fear of angry people. When someone is angry, we tend to take their anger personally. For example, at the medical staff meeting, Tom was hoping for help so that his patients would be safe. But he didn't know what he was feeling or why. Faster than conscious thought, his judge jumped in and blamed Sylvia for not doing her job. Tom appeared angry and verbally attacking, and at first Sylvia took it personally.

The good news is that when someone is upset, *we didn't cause their pain.* They want peace of mind; *they want their hope to be met.* They don't yet realize this consciously, but that doesn't matter, because we can help them to identify it.

First, we need to manage our own terror by centering ourselves. So we take a deep breath, as Sylvia did. We remember the apparent attack is not about us; it is a mistake to take it personally. The other person is angry because one of their hopes is not being met.

Then we guess at their feeling and hope: "Are you frustrated because you would like more support?"

This guess clearly demonstrates that we care about the other person's distress and that we are not judging them negatively. Their judge is disarmed. Our guess helps them shift from an unconscious blaming reaction to conscious thought. When they realize that their upset relates to their positive intention, they are pleased. There was no attack. What a relief to both parties!

The "because you" clause is crucial here. It links their feeling to their hope, showing that they really are not attacking but are upset about their unmet hope.

The other person is actually offering us, however inelegantly, a gift, an opportunity for us to help. If we hear anything but a gift in the other person's message, we haven't become conscious and heard them.

This is the difference between common empathy and true empathy. Common empathy is defined in the dictionary as "identification with and understanding of another's situation, feelings, and motives." When dealing with anger, this type of empathy means agreeing with the other person's judge. An example of common empathy would be "So you are angry because I treated you disrespectfully." Such a comment gives power to their judge's motive of blaming us for doing something wrong. By saying this we have accepted that we are the cause of the other person's upset. We may need to duck after saying it.

True empathy, on the other hand, is a conscious choice. We reach beyond other people's unconscious negative judgments and perceptions to connect with their real motives. Thus we say something on the order of, "Are you upset because you wanted (hope)?" To answer our guess the other person must shift his thinking to determine what he really wants. He lets go of his judge's blame and becomes more centered and conscious.

Most depression comes from being emotionally stuck. As we noted, the Latin root of emotion is motere, to move. Getting in touch with and expressing underlying pain and sadness moves and lifts depression. Learning to communicate helps men alleviate their depression, form relationships and find peaceful alternatives to violence.

Here is a classic example of listening consciously to an angry man.

Terry Dobson was studying the martial art, aikido, in Japan. His teacher had taught him: "Aikido is the art of reconciliation. Whoever has the mind to fight has broken his connection with the universe. If you try to dominate people, you are already defeated. We study how to resolve conflict, not how to start it."

One day when Terry was riding on a Tokyo train, a huge man, raging drunk, got on and began attacking and terrorizing the passengers. Terry felt called upon to intervene lest someone get seriously hurt. As all the other passengers sat frozen in their seats, Terry slowly stood up.

Seeing him, the drunk man roared, "Aha! A foreigner! You need a lesson in Japanese manners!" and he prepared to attack Terry.

At that moment someone loudly and joyously shouted: "Hey!" It had the cheery tone of one suddenly coming upon a good friend. The surprised drunk spun around to see a tiny Japanese man in his 70's beaming delight at him. With a wave of his hand and a happy "C'mere" the old man beckoned him over.

The drunk strode over and said, "Why the hell should I talk to you?"

"What'cha been drinking?" asked the old man, smiling.

"I've been drinking sake, and it's none of your business," bellowed the drunk.

"Oh, that's wonderful, absolutely wonderful," the old man replied warmly. "You see, I love sake too. Every night, me and my wife warm up a bottle of sake and take it out into the garden and we sit on an old wooden bench..." The old man continued on about this for a while. The drunk's face began to soften and his fists to unclench.

Then the old man said, "I'm sure you have a wonderful wife."

"No," said the drunk. "My wife died..." Sobbing, he launched into a sad tale of losing his wife, his home, his job, of being ashamed of himself.

By the time Terry got off the train the drunk was sprawled on the seat with his head on the old man's lap.

Where Terry would have attacked, the old man showed true empathy with the drunk's feelings and hopes, completely transforming the situation.

When I was in Switzerland, a Rwandan refugee, Georges, told me his story. His father had been murdered by neighbors in his village during the genocidal massacres. The Rwandan police had refused to help Georges bring the murderers to justice. The more he remembered this horrible time, the louder his voice got and the more his muscles tensed. "I must avenge this dishonor to my father," he pronounced with great force. I listened attentively to how angry he was at the killers, to his anguish at the injustice, to how frustrated he was when the higher police authorities laughed at him. After about fifteen minutes, he began to feel heard and gradually became calmer. I told him that I wished I'd been able to help him then. By the end of our session he said he no longer wanted to kill. Instead, he expressed his gratitude to me. This was one of my first experiences of the power of true empathy.

We can all do this, even when people appear to be angry at us. We first consciously override our judge's fear and remember, "I am OK; I can handle this. They are really not angry at me. They are just unable to identify and get empathy for their unmet hope. So I won't take it personally."

Then we help them by listening for these key elements:

		PURPOSE
Fact	"Are you reacting to...?"	clarifies starting point
Feeling	"Are you feeling upset because ?"	connects with their emotion
Hope	"Did you want...?"	identifies positive motivation
Request	"And now would you like...?"	shows easy way to agree

We quickly discover that their intention was positive. As they understand it with us, they return to a conscious, balanced state and become able to get their hope met.

Once we connect with the hope in another person, anger is removed, helping to restore inner peace. Frequently, however, as soon as the first upset has been resolved, the person becomes aware of an underlying feeling that is also connected to a hope. So we peel back the layers of feeling until they become more peaceful, lighter, or cease talking.

Transforming Our Anger – Getting True Empathy for Ourselves

Perhaps the greatest challenge we face as human beings is managing our own anger. Anger is a challenge because it is unavoidable and usually leads to some form of attack. Our judge generates anger the instant we perceive ourselves, or someone we care about, being threatened. Although our first feeling may be fear or sadness, our judge instantly projects responsibility for our feeling onto someone else. We attribute an evil motive to the other person, casting blame and wanting to make them pay.

Anger is the emotion that prepares our body and mind to attack. The hormonal rush makes it harder for us to think consciously, and therefore harder for us to change our mind.

Rarely is another person ready to rise above our angry attack. The other person's judge is in charge and not interested in our hope. Anger is tragic because it guarantees we will not get our hopes met. It prevents us from connecting with other people, destroying our relationships with them and with ourselves.

We feel sad after an outburst of anger because we have failed to see the goodness in the other person and failed to find it in ourselves.

But anger is transformable. Anger can be looked upon as a gift, because it wakes us up to a very important choice: to attack or to connect. Which choice will get us what we want? Which one is more powerful?

John Bargh offers a useful definition of power: "Power in a situation is the ability to attain your own personal goals." Our real goal in any interaction is to get our hopes met, not to attack. Hence, real power is not force. We cannot get our hopes met through coercion. Anger and the use of force only show that we believe we are weak. This is true powerlessness.

Power involves bringing forth hopes. Hopes and feelings are closer to our life energy than to our judgmental thoughts. They are more powerful. When we learn to identify and express our hopes in a non-coercive way, we discover great joy and freedom. I have repeatedly seen this satisfaction on people's faces in conscious communication workshops as connection validates their goodness and humanity.

Our thinking causes our anger. So to transform it we change our thinking, and, in so doing, we change how we feel. Here is how to do it:

Angry Thinking occurs when we think that a person has wronged or betrayed us. We see the other person as the problem and think they should be doing something else.

Imagine you are in the middle of telling Erica something and she leaves the room. This is a typical way to think about it:

Erica acted rudely toward me; she should have listened to what I had to say.

If you think of Erica as being rude to you and focus on what she did wrong, you are likely to feel angry toward her. And if you speak from your anger, "Erica, I feel hurt when you treat me rudely," Erica is likely to become defensive.

Conscious Thinking occurs when you focus on your unmet hopes:

I really wanted to be heard, to be respected, to have what I was saying considered.

Then you notice how you feel inside when you are not heard and you might feel sad. If you speak from this awareness and say, "Erica,

I feel sad because I really wanted to be heard," you are more likely to be listened to with compassion; Erica can hear your non-attacking invitation to meet your hope.

Consciously thinking about our own hopes is important, because when our hopes are not fulfilled, we have experienced a loss. The emotional response to loss is sadness, not anger. Expressing our sadness and hope heals our psyche and allows for resolution with the other person.

Here are four steps for transforming and using the energy of anger:

1. When you become aware of your anger, stop talking; become aware of yourself. Breathe. Center.

2. Notice your thinking; that you found something wrong about what the other person did. *I'm angry because this person should have....* Notice that you are blaming them for your feelings.

3. Forget about the other person and identify what you really wanted in the situation, your unmet hope: *I was hoping...*

   By identifying your unmet hope, you are giving yourself true empathy. This is a very powerful way to shift your consciousness to a deeper truth.

4. Notice how you feel now in relation to this hope not being met:

   When I focus on this unmet hope I feel....

And you discover the feeling that was beneath your anger.

Let's see how you might apply this process in your life.

Imagine that you work in a small company and Carolyn, the owner, asks you and three co-workers to come up with some creative ideas to improve the company's advertising. After putting a lot of thought into it, you have a sudden inspiration and write out a radio commercial. Your rework it several times and are extremely pleased with the result. Your spouse thinks it's terrific.

At the meeting with Carolyn your co-workers only come up with a few general suggestions about advertising. Then you run through your commercial and everybody laughs.

"That's great," says Carolyn. "Now, I'd like to tell you what I was thinking. Our best approach is to send out flyers with the local newspapers. I drafted these two samples and would like to get your feedback."

After the group has reviewed the flyers, Carolyn says, "Well, thanks a lot. Your feedback has been helpful."

Here is how you could transform your anger:

1. Notice you feel angry; pause and take a breath.

2. Become aware of what you're thinking, *She made a request and I came through with a great idea. She should have seriously considered my contribution.*

3. Now you shift your thinking from Carolyn to yourself. *What was I hoping? I was hoping to have my idea appreciated.*

4. Notice your new feeling. *I feel disappointed.*

Once you have transformed your anger, you have four options about how to proceed.

In this case it would be appropriate to:

- Speak your new feeling and hope to the person:

    "When... I feel... because I... and now will you...?"

    For example: "Carolyn, when you said, 'That's great,' and went on to discuss your idea, I felt disappointed because I was hoping to have my contribution acknowledged. Would you be willing to tell me if you see any value in it?

In another situation, if the other person is too upset to listen to you, you could

- Listen to the other person to discover their hope.

    "Carolyn, at the meeting were you feeling anxious because you really wanted to get the problem solved in a short time?"

If the situation is dangerous or if you are overwhelmed and need to replenish yourself by getting true empathy from a friend or from yourself, it would be wise to

- Leave

Or, if the situation is not that serious and you would like to lighten it up,

- Laugh

    "If we have more wacko meetings like that one, we should sell tickets."

Use the Anger Worksheet to practice transforming your anger in relation to a specific incident.

Marshall Rosenberg tells the following story, demonstrating what happens when we get in touch with the hope behind our anger. A facilitator was working with a group of prisoners and had just explained that our feelings are not solely the result of what someone else does.

One of the prisoners then asked, "What do you mean when you say that other people can't make you feel as you do?" The facilitator could tell from the look in the prisoner's eyes and the tone of his voice that the answer to this question was very important to him.

The facilitator said: "Think of a time recently that you had some angry feelings."

"I'm really angry at the prison staff," the prisoner replied.

The facilitator asked what was making him so angry.

"I asked them three weeks ago whether I could do a certain kind

ANGER WORKSHEET

1.   I felt angry when (describe what the other person did or did not do).

   _____

   _____

   _____

2.   In this situation I was angry because I was thinking the other person
      should have

   _____

   _____

   _____

Now mentally erase the other person and shift your thinking to inside yourself.

3.   In this situation my general hope was _____

   _____

   _____

4.   When my attention is on this hope, and I think of it not being met,
      what feeling do I experience? _____

   _____

   _____

Now complete a statement about the same event from your new perspective:

When _____

I felt _____

   _____

Because I _____

   _____

of training and they haven't given me an answer yet."

The facilitator said, "Your answer makes it sound as though their lack of response to your request is the sole source of your anger."

"It is," the prisoner said.

"I'm concerned about your saying that they are the cause of your anger. I'd like you to look at what is going on in you that is also contributing to the anger."

He asked, "What do you mean?"

The facilitator said, "Tell me what you are thinking about the staff not giving you an answer yet about the training."

"It's typical of some of the staff," he replied. "They are totally insensitive to the needs of the prisoners. They treat us as though we don't exist."

The facilitator said, "I believe it's these things you are telling yourself about the staff that are making you angry and not simply what the staff is doing. Do you see what I mean?"

"How should I think about it?" he asked.

The facilitator replied, "Anytime you are angry I believe you will find that it is because you are thinking in judgmental terms about what others are doing. In one way or another you are thinking that they are wrong and shouldn't be doing what they are doing."

"How else can I think about it?"

The facilitator replied, "I'd like to show you what happens when you focus your attention on your unmet needs rather than on interpreting others' actions. Focus your attention now on what you would like in this situation that you are not getting and tell me what this is."

"I need the training I requested because the work I want to do when I get out of here depends on my having the training. If I don't have that training, I'm likely to end up back in here shortly after I get out."

The facilitator said, "Now that your attention is focused on your need to have a good job and retain your freedom, tell me how you feel when you think of not getting it."

"I feel scared," the prisoner said.

"Notice that when your attention is focused on your unfulfilled desires, you feel scared. When your attention is directed to judging what is wrong with the staff for not fulfilling your needs, you feel angry."

At that moment the young man looked very sad and hung his head. The facilitator asked, "What's going on?"

The prisoner said, "If I could have sorted out what was going on inside me two years ago, I wouldn't have killed my best friend."

Anger is a symptom of our judge's attempt to cast blame on someone, to make someone pay or feel guilty. It is based on misinterpretation. Anger leads only to attack, which guarantees we will not get our hopes met. It also prevents us from connecting with other people. Fortunately, when we experience anger, we can transform the energy for our positive use by shifting our attention to our unmet hopes.

Speaking Powerfully – Getting True Empathy from Others

"I will not be a doormat!" "Enough listening to the other guy; how do I get satisfaction in a conflict?" "Why are other people so defensive?" "What if they don't know how to listen to me?" These questions come up in workshops all the time, and they must be answered.

Giving up our anger does not leave us as a victim or "doormat" without a voice. On the contrary it gives us the only effective way to get our hopes met—speaking assertively from our passion, from the power of our feelings and hopes. Let's look at an example.

Lorraine had been feeling helpless at work for months. As Nurse Manager of a large medical practice, she regularly had to interact with a high-powered physician, Dr. Walters, who frequently criticized her and her nursing staff. His loud, angry outbursts were very intimidating. After taking the conscious communication program, Lorraine decided she had the tools she needed to confront him effectively.

She set up a meeting with Dr. Walters in her office. Prior to the meeting, Lorraine reflected on her hopes: to make a genuine connection with Dr. Walters, to remain centered in spite of his angry criticisms of her, to be treated respectfully and to have her staff treated respectfully. Here, slightly condensed, is their conversation:

Their Words	Communication Elements
Lorraine: "I asked to talk with you today because I would like to work together for the well-being of our patients. I want us to be on the same team, and when I hear you say that the staff here doesn't do a good job, I feel upset."	Opener Fact Feeling
Dr. Walters: "Well, frankly, the care here isn't what it should be. People aren't doing things correctly. You need to train your people better and supervise them more closely."	Blame
Lorraine: "I understand you would like to see more supervision. Actually, the charge nurses increased their supervision hours starting last week. I'm working on several projects that will ultimately provide more and better training."	Hearing his hope Supplying information
"But when you criticize the staff in front of the patients, I feel very upset. I need you to respect me and my staff."	Fact Feeling Hope

Dr. Walters: "I just don't like what I see. I don't think you are effectively maintaining standards. What do you do anyway?"

Blame

Lorraine took a deep breath, thought about what his hopes might be behind his attacking words. Then she began by acknowledging what she thought was important to him.

Centering

Lorraine: "Dr. Walters, you are a very exacting physician and you give excellent care to our patients. We both want what is best for our patients, and unless we work together, it will be difficult to achieve that goal. My staff needs to be treated with respect. When you have concerns and you bring them straight to the Medical Director, instead of to me, I feel frustrated."

His values

Commonality of hopes.

Hope
Fact

Feeling

Dr. Walters: "I do that because you have to ask him about everything anyway."

Attack

Lorraine: "I'd like it if you would speak directly to me. I need you to understand the way the system works, for you to be respectful of it and of my position. Your standards are important, and working together we can maintain them."

Request
Hope

Hope

Dr. Walters: "It's not just you and your nursing staff I'm upset with. I don't really like the way things are done by the other physicians in the practice either.

Disclosure

So it's not just the nursing staff. I just won't compromise on my standards!"	Hope
Lorraine: "Dr. Walters, are you unhappy with the group you're working with?"	Guessing at feeling
Dr. Walters: "I'm not happy with a lot of things."	Feeling
Lorraine: "I appreciate that you have high standards when it comes to our patients. I share those same high standards. I would never expect you to compromise your principles. Can you work with us to achieve quality care? Would you be willing to do some training with the staff? Would you be willing to meet at the beginning of your rotation so I can fill you in on what has been going on in the unit, and at the end of the month so you can give me feedback? This would allow us to keep each other informed of important issues and concerns."	Hearing hope

Hope
Request

Request |
| Dr. Walters: "Yes, I think that would be helpful." And he reached out and shook hands with Lorraine. | Empathy |

Lorraine was delighted. She and Dr. Walters met regularly thereafter. They began to share on a professional level and it wasn't long before she felt the respect she wanted for herself and for her staff. The benefits of their newfound cooperation led to a more positive atmosphere in the unit for staff and patients alike.

Lorraine successfully confronted Dr. Walters, sidestepped his attacks, and won his respect and cooperation. As Lorraine reflected on the conversation, she realized he was initially too angry to hear her. It wasn't until she let him know that she heard his feelings and hopes that they could really talk.

We may find ourselves in a situation in which we want very badly to influence someone, yet the other person doesn't seem to hear us or care. At such a time we may "shout" in conscious communication to bring the other person's attention to our hope. Assertive communication involves a concise and strong expression of our feelings and hopes. We use emphatic language, tone, volume, eye contact and gestures to let the other person know the strength of our feeling and hope.

For example, let's imagine that you found drugs in your 16-year-old son's room. You might "shout:"

You: "I'm really scared about this, Ben! Let's talk about it."

Son: "What's the big deal?"

You: "I'm afraid you could die and I really love you."

Your "shout" is your emphatic statement of your feeling and/or hope.

Insisting on true empathy

After we have expressed ourselves to another person, we want to know that our feelings and hopes were heard and heard accurately. We want empathic understanding. We need it for our emotions to return to center. To get it we might say something like "How did you hear what I said?"

For example, if after you said, "I'm afraid you could die and I really love you," your son said, "Hey Mom, I'm OK. I've got to go meet a friend now," connection at the level of feelings and hopes has not occurred. So you insist on it by saying:

"This is important to me. I need to know that you have heard what I'm saying. I said, "I'm afraid you could die and I really love you." Will you please tell me what you heard me say?"

"Yeah, you're worried about me, but you don't need to be. Can I go now?"

"No, that's not what I said. I'm not just worried. I said, "I'm afraid you could die and I really love you." What did you hear me say?"

"You said you were afraid I might die and you love me."

"Yes. Thank you."

When your son said, "You said you were afraid I might die and you love me," something shifted. He could no longer brush you off. By saying it, he has understood it. Communication has occurred. You have both been brought closer to conscious center. You insisted on and received true empathy.

When we need true empathy, we persist until the other person is able to repeat our feeling and hope to our satisfaction, we thank them and then ask them how they feel when they hear us say that. In this way we can find out their feelings and hopes. When both people's feelings and hopes are kept present we can find solutions.

Saying "no"

Another important assertive communication skill is being able to say "no" without having it sound like a negative judgment. Here is the problem: Saying "no" is saying what we don't want and the other person feels unwanted, rejected.

Imagine a friend has made this request of you: "I'd like to stop by tonight and tell you what's been going on in my relationship." Here is how you might say "no" while being conscious not to be negative:

1) Demonstrate empathy with the request being made.

"It sounds like you're concerned about your relationship and want to talk."

2) Express the hope that is preventing you from saying "yes."

"I've been really strung out and need time this evening to take care of myself."

3) Connect with the other person in a way that indicates your openness to problem solving until both can find a way to fulfill their hopes.

"Could we find another time to get together?"

This establishes connection and is more communicative than saying "No, you may not come over and talk." The other person's hope has not been rejected; they just have to get it met in a different way or different time.

We have seen the power of true empathy in transforming anger and as a way of asserting ourselves without attacking. But in some cases we may have lingering doubts about its applicability. We may think, "Aren't there some people and actions that really are so awful that we don't want to extend empathy?"

This is the most important question a human being needs to answer:
"Is the universe a friendly place or not?"

– ALBERT EINSTEIN

CHAPTER EIGHT

Forgiveness

You may have experienced that it is difficult to give up your anger, especially when you feel badly hurt. How can you simply "mentally erase" the other person? You may think, "There are some people, some acts, that I simply can't forget." Here are two specific thoughts that are hard to let go of after a serious conflict:

- The other person did it intentionally.
- The hurt was so great as to be irreparable.

When we think these thoughts, we feel resentment, anger, even rage. We are certain that conscious communication can't change this situation. Yet we also know that anger and resentment poison our bodies and lock us into judge consciousness. We can't change what we see as the facts of the matter, so we're stuck. And the thought that the perpetrator of our hurt has the power to continue to make us miserable in this way, robbing our life of joy, may cause us to feel even angrier. We are not the perpetrator! We are innocent! We feel frustrated and powerless.

To make matters worse, part of us knows we should be acting more nobly, loving our neighbor as ourselves. The world's major religious and spiritual teachings seem to agree on this, as seen in Table 13.

I, too, have experienced major wrongs and become very angry about them. I felt justified in my anger and self-righteous in my desire to see the perpetrator punished. When I compare my thinking to the golden rule, I get confused. Either there are plenty of exceptions to the golden rule or I am petty and not able to attain this standard.

We need to move beyond the surface of the golden rule and understand the profound lesson it is teaching us. The lesson centers on the two ways of looking at forgiveness.

Common Forgiveness Keeps Us Stuck

In order to let go of our anger we must forgive. The Germanic roots of the word forgive are "far," meaning "away" and "geban," meaning "to give." To forgive means to "give up" or "leave off," to stop trying to be right about what is wrong with the other person. To forgive we must completely overlook any perception of bad or evil intention, any wrongdoing or sin on the part of the other person.

What then do we do with our mind? Go blank? We all know this doesn't work. To forgive we must find the good. To forgive is to let go of blame completely by replacing it with recognition of goodness.

In the English language today, however, the word forgive has two meanings. The first meaning in the dictionary is "to excuse for a fault or an offense; to pardon." I will refer to this as common forgiveness, a judge's interpretation. It implies that the other person did indeed do something wrong, which we, because we are morally above the other person, deign not to punish them for, at least for now. We do, however, save their transgression in memory to bring up the next time we want to coerce them with guilt. We don't see their error as a simple mistake, but as an intended evil act, making the other person different from and less than we are.

This is an insidious judge trick. Our judge is saying to the other person "I am so good (and so superior), I won't hold your badness against you." Naturally, our judgment brings about a defensive reaction in them. But that is only part of the damage. If people are essentially the same, any time we see badness or evil in another person, we are seeing it in ourselves.

Table 13 – **The Golden Rule in World Religions**

One should always treat others as they themselves wish to be treated.	**Hinduism**
Thou shalt love thy neighbor as thyself.	**Judaism**
Whatever is disagreeable to yourself do not do unto others.	**Zoroastrianism**
Hurt not others with that which pains you.	**Buddhism**
What you do not want done to yourself do not do to others.	**Confucianism**
Whatever you wish that others would do to you, do so to them.	**Christianity**
No one of you is a believer until he loves for his neighbor what he loves for himself.	**Islam**

Is it possible to really forgive a hurt that we are certain someone inflicted on us? The psychology of common forgiveness rests on our expectation of external threat. When we expect threat, that is what we see. Our defensive reaction then provokes the other person to react defensively, creating a self-fulfilling prophecy. In this way we create and sustain a threatening psychological reality in which we see the other person as blameworthy.

When we blame someone, we want them to know they are responsible for doing something bad. If they did something bad, then they are bad, and we want them to suffer in their wrongness. "Punishment" is inflicting a hurtful penalty for wrongdoing, and we see punishment as a justified attack on the wrongdoer.

Here is a psychological truth your judge doesn't like to admit—punishing someone is like setting off a bomb in a closed space—it harms both parties.

When we seek to punish someone we harm ourselves because we are using attack as self-defense. When we choose to attack we are choosing to be cruel as protection from what we fear. This has two disastrous psychological effects on us.

First, instead of reducing our fear, our fear grows. When we defend against threats we legitimize them. Seeing a need to protect ourselves, we value being vigilant in our perceiving of threatening people and their actions before they hurt us. And we find what we are looking for. As we see more threats, we need greater defenses.

Second, when we chose to be cruel, we have cashiered our self-image of being good. Good people don't attack and hurt other people. We can rationalize till the cows come home, saying the other person is worse than we are, and therefore deserves to be punished. But we can't change the fact that we have chosen to be cruel.

Throwing blame bombs may not hurt the other guy in the slightest. If he sees himself as the innocent victim of your attack, his psychological well-being remains unharmed.

A bomb thrower is a bomb thrower, whether he throws large or small bombs. Common forgiveness involves negatively judging someone for a wrong (throwing a small bomb) and graciously not hitting them with a penalty. We then say to ourselves, "See how good I am by not dropping the big bomb that bad person really deserves." The psychological stress from attempting to maintain the façade of being good while being cruel can keep us up at night.

But this is the path our judges take. If we don't direct them, our judges follow beliefs inherited from the collective unconscious. When they make negative judgments, they do so with our tacit approval. Unfortunately, this reinforces our belief in an unfriendly universe, and we continue to blame others and to sabotage our relationships.

Each time we fail to reverse a negative judgment, we are opting to remain in an attacking mode. Then forgiveness is not possible because we are saving the other person's wrongs as proof of their badness. They become weapons in our attacks.

We are stuck in a vicious cycle. The root of the problem lies deep inside us, in two core beliefs of the collective unconscious that we have come to hold about ourselves:

- We believe we are vulnerable.

- We believe we are powerless.

It is these unconscious beliefs about ourselves that give rise to our fearful defensiveness. What can we do about it? Albert Einstein said that a problem cannot be solved with the kind of thinking that created the problem.

The Two Levels

We can learn to see the universe as friendly and ourselves as invulnerable by changing our ideas about who we are. The beliefs that we are vulnerable and powerless stem from the idea that we are bodies. This idea is only partly true. Our bodies are the houses of our unconscious minds.

Candace Pert, Ph.D., author of *Molecules of Emotion: Why You Feel the Way You Feel*, describes the network of peptides and receptors that make up the body's information and emotional systems. Her research proves that information is processed not only in the brain, but also in "nodal points" throughout the body, each containing many receptors. These nodal points process our sense information, filter it, prioritize it, and bias it, causing chemical and emotional changes in us. In this way the body causes our emotions and our perceptions. Our emotions decide what is worth paying attention to and regulate what we experience as reality. Dr. Pert states "The body is our unconscious mind."

Bodily reality is the unconscious world we inhabit 99% of the time. The judge is perfectly at home here. Bodies are not the same; they are obviously different one from another and the judge delights in judging them. Bodies can attack and hurt other bodies. If we see ourselves as only bodies we see ourselves as vulnerable to attack. The unconscious is a familiar, but not a safe or pleasant neighborhood in which to live. Where then, is our conscious mind?

Spirit is defined as "the vital principle or animating force within living beings; incorporeal consciousness." Incorporeal means "lacking material form." So, by definition, the source of conscious thought is not in the body. Our conscious minds are not stuck in our bodies. "I have a body, but I am not my body. I am more than that. I am the one who is aware."

Have you ever had an experience of being at one with the universe? Almost everyone can remember a moment of blissful unity. It might have been a peaceful time alone in a natural setting, or it might have been an instant of full connection with another person. These experiences of pure consciousness leave us with an indescribable feeling of wonder and joy at the mystery of life. They give us a sense of the spiritual.

What if spirit is who we really are? This is a way of thinking about our lives that can help our self-image and our relationships enormously. We are in the habit of believing we are essentially bodies. What if we see ourselves as essentially spirit? The belief that we are spirit has helped many people to forgive others completely and see the universe as friendly. To say we are essentially spirit is to say that we acknowledge a life force in us that is more than our bodies.

Imagine spirit is the essential, invisible level at which all of us are good and the same. Because spirit has no physical form, it cannot attack and cannot be hurt. Spirit cannot fear; it can only love. As spirit, we are invulnerable.

Let's look at the merits of this belief as a mental tool, a personal choice. We are interested in resolving conflicts and building relationships. Let's assume for the moment that we are willing to consider the possibility of consciously adopting the belief that we are spirit. What are the advantages and disadvantages to building relationships?

Here are some advantages we can assume if we believe that we are essentially spirit:

- Because spirit is invulnerable, we cannot experience harm and so we cannot be threatened.

- Because spirit is eternal, we do not die; only the body dies.

Here is the main disadvantage:

- If we talk about being essentially spirit, people with a non-religious/non-spiritual orientation will think we are crazy.

Arguments that we are spirit are unlikely to convince us. The most powerful learning tool is practical experience. We have to try this out to see if it works.

Robert Gass, a man who believes implicitly in his reality as spirit told me this story. One winter, he rented a Winnebago in San Diego to go on vacation with his wife and small daughter. He spoke some Spanish and was looking forward to experiencing the cactus-strewn deserts of Mexico's western coast.

One evening the family found themselves in a beautiful spot on the beach with pink mesas on one side and the sun setting over the Pacific on the other. There was no town or RV park for miles, and the place was so serene they decided to camp there.

Late that night four men burst into their Winnebago shouting for money. They were brandishing a rifle and large knives. Robert was terrified, especially for his wife and wide-eyed child sitting on her bunk. How could he safely force these intruders out? The leader, apparently reading his mind, moved closer to the little girl. Robert took a deep breath. Then he took out his wallet and handed it over.

The leader yelled for more, wafting Robert with the smell of beer. Robert located his wife's purse and gave the bandits her money. As he did this he took a closer look at the men. They were young and one of them hung back, darting glances at the leader for direction. Robert smiled at him, took off his watch and wedding ring, and handed them to him. The young man's hand was shaking.

"Mas!" cried the leader. Robert looked at him, gave an obedient nod, went to a small drawer, took out his wife's jewelry and handed it over. Robert then signed to his wife to take off and give them her wedding ring and watch, which she did.

Robert put his hand to his chin for a second. "Mi cámara," he said. He uncovered his camera, which was hanging under a jacket, and turned it over.

Then, smiling, he folded down a table. He went to the little refrigerator and took out beer and food. While they watched he opened the beers, handed one to each man and began making them sandwiches. He asked them to sit down. One sat; the others stood. Robert found them a canvas bag for their loot and threw in a radio.

In a jovial tone, Robert told them some of the beautiful sights his family had seen in Mexico and saw some recognition on their faces. He asked them where else was pretty and one of them said "La Bufadora." He asked the man to tell him about it. As they talked, ate and drank, everybody relaxed. Robert asked them how to get to La Bufadora and one of them pointed a direction. Robert wasn't clear and asked the man to show him outside. Outside Robert was surprised to see they had no vehicle.

Robert offered them a ride. They looked at each other and the leader said he would tell him where to drive. Robert bumped the Winnebago along dirt roads for a while until told to halt. As they got out Robert handed one of them a box of cookies. They all bid each other "adios." When the door closed Robert sat on his daughter's bed and they had a family hug.

A few minutes later there was a knock on the door. It was one of the young men.

"I am sorry," he said, handing back his credit cards, wedding rings, and some of the money. "You are a good man. I hope you enjoy Mexico."

"*Muchas gracias, amigo,*" Robert replied. "*Adios.*" He heard them laughing as they walked off into the night.

On a bodily level Robert and his family were vulnerable. But Robert's belief that he is essentially spirit was reflected in his free and loving behavior. By letting them see that he did not feel threatened by them, Robert communicated to the men that they were good and they were grateful to be seen that way.

The idea that people are essentially spirit can help us in conscious communication. While this assumption is not required in order to communicate consciously, it can facilitate taking the leap of faith that we make when we deny our perception and guess at the other person's hope.

Theology is an area in which the judge's judgments really go to town. Religious training comes to us largely through the collective unconscious and from early parental teaching. While much of it, such as the golden rule, can be helpful in awakening us to the truth that people are essentially good and the same; religious doctrine, in attempting to make abstract truths specific, has often provided ammunition to the judge, whose goal is to find difference and judge some of those differences as bad.

We will never all have the same theology, but we can have the same experience of giving and receiving love. It is toward this experience that this book is directed—the universal experience of loving our neighbor as ourselves. Seeing people as spirit is a mental tool that allows us to see ourselves as invulnerable and unable to be threatened. In this way we recognize the universe as friendly. Thus we have nothing to fear and we do not need to change other people. We only need to see who they really are, spirits, beings of pure love, seeking to be recognized.

This answers the problem of believing we are vulnerable. How about the problem of believing we are weak and powerless?

The Power of Love

The golden rule is powered by love. As we act according to the golden rule, love helps us. Love—a deep, tender, ineffable feeling of affection and solicitude toward a person, such as that arising from kinship, recognition of attractive qualities, or a sense of underlying oneness— accepts others as good and the same. "Ineffable" means incapable of being described; we can't prove love exists, so it falls in the spiritual realm. But we know from our experience that love improves our sense of well-being and our world view.

If we don't feel the power to love, how do we get it? From another person? Then the golden rule is backwards and we need other people to love us. No. The rule is exact. And the rule holds the secret that will set us free.

We create love and learn to love ourselves as we extend love to others. When we take the leap of faith and choose to extend positive understanding to someone, love appears.

This indirect creation of love frequently amazes us. As soon as we let go of the judge's trapeze and guess at hopes, love's invisible hands connect us securely to the hands of the other person and we both swing to safety.

After lovingly resolving a conflict, we feel happy, peaceful, and fulfilled. Our feelings, plus the obvious satisfaction experienced by the other person, let us know that we gave love, and we can only give what we have. Hence we realize that we are vehicles for love. Love flows through us the instant we choose to connect rather than defend.

By giving love we create it. This is a miracle. Knowledge of who we really are allows us to take the leap of faith. The more often we leap, the more we connect. The belief that we are spirit and can summon the power of love helps us to forgive completely.

Complete Forgiveness Empowers Us

The second meaning of forgiveness in the dictionary is "to renounce anger or resentment against." This is complete forgiveness. Complete forgiveness is our key to creating a friendly universe. This is what we do when we practice conscious override.

The concept that we are spirit frees us from our dilemma of the intentional or irreparable hurt. It gives us a way to see that the "wrong" never hurt our spirit, never hurt who we really are. As spirit we are loving and invulnerable. The worst that happened was that the other person's judge made a mistake.

This view allows us to realize that an action we initially perceived as bad need not be seen as irrevocably harmful. Instead, we can use conscious override to hear the good in another person. To forgive is to know that no real harm was done and none was really intended. In this way we completely renounce our anger and resentment. Complete forgiveness heals the other person and ourselves. We have identified with love rather than cruelty.

Being Practical

Generally we don't make a great once-and-for-all decision about forgiveness. We make this choice moment by moment in each interaction we have with other people. By now we know if we wait to see if the people with whom we are in conflict are good or bad, our judges will prove them bad, so at the first alarm we use conscious override.

Naturally we wonder if the assumption that people are essentially good and motivated by positive intentions always holds.

There have been several moving articles in periodicals in the last few years describing how the desire to connect empathically is just beneath the surface in men who have killed someone. What these men's conscious selves crave is to share their sadness and remorse with those who have been hurt so they can be seen for who they really were. They want to express their sadness at the huge mistake they made. When this occurs they heal, and so do the families of the victims.

As Dr. Jasper Becker was driving his family home from the movies, a sports car smashed into his van and overturned it. His wife, Kathy Becker, was trapped inside the van. Repeatedly she called her daughter's name but got no answer. Seventeen-year-old Loren was dead. The driver of the sports car fled the scene but was later arrested.

"Human language is inadequate to express the anguish and emptiness I experienced during the ensuing weeks," Kathy reported "I felt I had lost Loren forever. Nothing would ever be the same."

Yet when Kathy learned the teenage driver was emotionally devastated, rocking back and forth in the fetal position, she saw an innocent child. She forgave him, and as she did, "A wave of love washed over me. A huge burden evaporated from my shoulders. I felt lighter. The grief shifted. I still missed Loren. I still wanted her back. But... forgiving Jorge meant that I did not have to live the rest of my life filled with blaming and bitterness. It also made it easier for Jorge to forgive himself."

Jorge, who had thought Kathy wanted to kill him, said, "She wanted to help me. I felt a weight lift off me—she didn't hate me! I felt human again." Kathy urged the court for leniency and after serving a year in jail, Jorge went to college.

This is the result of complete forgiveness—joyful inner peace coupled with the realization that we are essentially loving beings.

What, then, do we do with people who do bad things? We forgive them. Yes, we certainly get them off the street and prevent them from harming others, but we do so without anger and vengeance. To heal them and to heal ourselves, we connect with their conscious selves so they can wake up and recognize they are good and loving. They may have made mistakes, but spirits don't get hurt or die and it is never too late to wake up and experience love.

Archbishop Desmond Tutu of South Africa believes in the principle that people are essentially the same and interconnected, that "my humanity is caught up in your humanity." As chairman of the Truth and Reconciliation Commission he recently said, "Reconciliation, forgiveness, confession are not the normal currency of politics," but "if you are in earnest about a catharsis, a therapeutic experience ... it's healing of memories, it's healing of attitudes, it's healing of heart, it's healing of spirit. Any other kind [of process] would be superficial, would be almost spurious, if not positively dangerous."

Our daily challenge isn't with killers. It's with our family and friends. Love is reality. As we forgive another person, we experience this truth of love, peace and joy. We join Albert Einstein in a friendly world.

Forgiveness occurs first in the mind, the instant we make the leap of faith to guess at the other person's hope. To learn to forgive we practice changing our attitude about other people. We can do this in our own minds with the following two exercises:

Reflective Forgiveness Exercise

Thinking of ither person,

1. List this person's "wrongs" quickly as they come to mind, all the evil things you have thought of them.

2. Put yourself in their situation. Imagine you did what they did. What were your hopes? Now consider each thing you did and honestly ask yourself, "Would I condemn myself for doing this?" You may have been inept, but you do not deserve horrendous punishment.

3. Now let the other person be free of all thoughts you had of wrongdoing in them.

4. Notice how you feel relieved and more relaxed.

When we put ourselves in other people's shoes, we can more easily imagine that their behavior could spring from limited perception and limited awareness of options, rather than from evil intent.

Some of us learn better through a visual process.

Visual Forgiveness Exercise

1. Think of someone you do not like, who seems to irritate you.

2. Try to perceive some light in them somewhere, a little gleam.

3. Let this light extend until it covers them.

4. Imagine them offering you this light.

5. See yourselves mutually blessing each other.

We can practice these exercises alone in quiet moments. They are a useful supplement to conscious communication.

Interactive Practice of Forgiveness

Through the conscious listening process, we see and hear only another person's positive intention. We give them true empathy. They want to communicate their hopes, but are limited in their ability to consciously recognize them.

Acting as the person who is temporarily saner in a conflict situation, we can shift the misperceptions for both parties. We don't call attention to a mistake and then pretend to pardon it. We have seen that is just our judge's attempt to be superior to the other person. Rather, we choose to see only the truth: the love or the call for help.

The best way to learn to love ourselves and others is to have the experience of giving and receiving love. The hundreds of people with whom I've worked in communication workshops make a single statement: the way to heal relationships is to forgive through conscious communication. This fills our lives with love.

The Table 14 summarizes our discussion.

Table 14 – **Forgiveness**

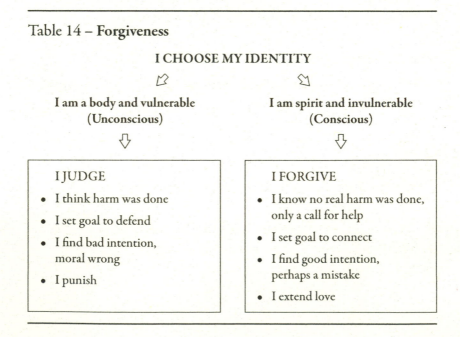

I CHOOSE MY IDENTITY

I am a body and vulnerable (Unconscious)	I am spirit and invulnerable (Conscious)
I JUDGE • I think harm was done • I set goal to defend • I find bad intention, moral wrong • I punish	**I FORGIVE** • I know no real harm was done, only a call for help • I set goal to connect • I find good intention, perhaps a mistake • I extend love

If your happiness depends on what somebody else does...
you do have a problem.

– RICHARD BACH

CHAPTER NINE

Creating Joyful Intimate Relationships

The quality of our intimate relationships determines the quality of our lives. No area is more important. Dr. John Cacioppo, a psychologist at Ohio State University, found that "It's the most important relationships in your life, the people you see day in and day out, that seem to be crucial to your health. And the more significant the relationship is in your life, the more it matters for your health." Yet no area has more false judge assumptions leading to self-sabotage and tragic, unnecessary misunderstandings.

Our primary relationship is a mirror of our state of mind. Our thoughts determine the nature of our interactions with our partner, so let us first look at the false assumptions we hold about relationships. We must know what we are thinking that is not helpful. Then we can recognize it. Once our thinking is changed, we can revise our behavior and attain positive results.

Five Damaging Assumptions in Relationships

On our first trip together as a step family, Elizabeth, Evan and I went to Washington, D.C. As we headed into town on the metro I was reading about Thomas Jefferson in a guidebook. Later, at the Jefferson Memorial, I overheard Elizabeth say to Evan, "Jefferson wrote the Declaration of Independence."

I added, "Jefferson was the primary author, but the Declaration was drafted by a committee that included John Adams, Benjamin Franklin and a couple others."

A few minutes later Elizabeth told Evan "Jefferson was a brilliant scholar and scientist. President Reagan once told a visiting group of Nobel Prize winners that they were the most impressive pool of talent at the White House since Jefferson dined there alone."

I jumped in again, "Actually, it was Kennedy who said that, not Reagan."

A few more times that morning I imparted my wisdom. The next time we were alone Elizabeth said to me "I don't like it when you correct me in front of Evan all the time."

"But," I pleaded, "I don't want him to have the wrong information."

"Look, Andy, Evan and I don't know each other very well yet and I'm trying to share with him to build a relationship. When you correct me all the time I feel irritated. It makes me seem less competent and teaches Evan he doesn't have to take women seriously. What are you trying to do here?"

I remembered that my main reason for going on the trip was so we could all grow together as a family. I had been unconsciously sabotaging that goal. My judge was back to his old tricks, finding little faults. When I am unconscious, my judge's priorities prevail. I had fallen prey to the first false assumption.

First False Relationship Assumption: I am conscious.

I was embarrassed when I realized what I had been doing to Elizabeth, but now I had a choice. I could continue to be right about names and dates or I could give her some space to build a happy family. I apologized and told her I would be glad to stop correcting her in front of Evan.

We can choose to become conscious at any time. Whoever is saner in the moment can do it. We can see this by reviewing a story from Chapter 6. Amanda was reading her magazine and David walked by without speaking. Amanda originally said, "I feel hurt when you ignore me. Why don't you talk to me?" He heard it as an attack. If David had been familiar with conscious communication, he could have centered himself as soon as he noticed his irritation and chosen to become conscious. Then he could have guessed at what was going on inside Amanda:

"When I went into the garage were you disappointed because you wanted to talk?"

Amanda would probably have replied, "Well, yes, I did want us to spend some time getting close this weekend." Now David knows that her intention is not to criticize him but to get closer to him.

The solution is to stop, center, and think "What do I really want to come out of this situation in terms of my hopes?"

We then override our judges and change our goal to connection, guiding our thoughts and actions so we get what we really want. Experiencing the peace and joy that come from being in harmony with the other person we realize, "Oh yes, this is what I really wanted."

The other day my neck was stiff and I wanted a massage. I said to Elizabeth, "My neck is really stiff."

"Oh? I'm sorry to hear that," she replied.

I felt disappointed. I wanted her to offer to give me a massage. My thinking went like this: *I offer to massage her neck all the time. This isn't fair.* But I had not told her what I wanted.

Second False Relationship Assumption: My partner knows what I want.

Instead of holding on to my resentment, I asked Elizabeth for a massage and she said, "Sure."

What do we do when the stakes are bigger and our partner says, "No"?

Christine ran a small business with her husband and he had been in the habit of telling her what to do for twenty years. Being consistently overruled was finally getting to Christine. She had found over the years that she couldn't win arguments with him and had given up trying. Now she felt so oppressed she couldn't stand it. She was ready to explode. Fortunately, she came to a conscious communication program where she learned the art of confronting powerfully without attacking.

In role-play Christine practiced saying "I want my wishes to be considered," and "I want to be treated with respect." Then she went home and tried these phrases on her husband.

At our next session she reported that her husband had refused her loudly and stubbornly at first. But after a while, in the face of her sincere persistence, he listened to what she wanted. He then agreed to go along with her business idea and gained a new admiration for her. She gained respect for herself at the same time. Christine had not only salvaged her marriage and business partnership, she began rejuvenating them.

In intimate relationships we often expect our partner to know what it is we want without our telling them, without making sure they have heard us. We think that if they love me they'll know what I want. We assume that the other person is able to discern what we want but just won't do it for us because they are mean or defective.

We have an inaccurate view of love. We think that love is something that gives them insight into us. We think it is their job to perceive and lovingly meet our hopes and needs. Our sense of belonging hinges on what they do for us. But then, when they innocently do something that doesn't meet our hopes, we are horribly let down and disappointed. Our judge determines their inadequacy. This locks us into judge-consciousness and we sabotage the opportunity to have our hopes met. We end up feeling sad or angry.

The solution begins by consciously giving up an unrealistic expectation that our partner should read our mind. Instead we verbalize an opportunity for them to contribute to our well-being. We let our partner know our hope and give them a specific way to help us meet it by making a clear request.

Solution: Tell my partner what I am feeling and hoping and give them the opportunity to help me.

Newlywed Barbara shared with our conscious communication group that since her honeymoon she had been miserable and full of self-doubt. Every day when her husband got off work he went out for beer with the guys. He came home late in no shape to relate intimately. She had told him she wanted to be able to talk and share with him, and without this connection she was very unhappy.

Third False Relationship Assumption: My partner will meet all my needs

Corollary: I must sacrifice to meet my partner's needs.

Talk about slavery! This assumption causes us immense suffering. It is tragic because our intention is often good—that we'll help each other—but our way of going about it dooms us to failure, so neither of us gets our hopes met. We expect and even demand that our partner meet all our needs.

In the communication program Barbara learned how to talk with her husband at a deeper level, and she heard what he really wanted. Drinking with his friends after work was very important to him, more important than coming home to share with her. The daily beer routine gave him a feeling of freedom and shared camaraderie. Barbara didn't attack him for his preferences. They both realized their marriage didn't meet their different hopes and agreed to divorce with no hard feelings. Barbara saved herself years of working on a relationship that would never meet her hopes. After her divorce she was free to seek emotional understanding and satisfaction from a new partner.

An important thing to note here is that Barbara didn't just decide to dump her husband. She mustered her courage and disclosed her hopes to him. She also took the time to discover and validate his hopes. Hopes are only good. Perhaps her husband was unskilled in how to get his freedom and companionship hopes met. In any case, she met an obligation that we all owe to ourselves and to our partners—to fully explore both people's hopes before deciding that they can't be met in the relationship.

Had Barbara tried to coerce her husband into changing at a fundamental level, into moving in a direction in which he was either not interested or too afraid to go, she would have done worse than waste her time. She would have been asking him to make a sacrifice. And sacrifice breeds resentment.

When we are fearful that we don't have enough and want our partner to suffer loss so we might gain, we are not thinking consciously. We cannot gain by taking something away from someone else. Would Barbara really have wanted her husband to come straight home resenting her? With sacrifice, neither person gets their hopes met.

The assumption that our partner must meet all our needs is a subset of the judge's chief premise: there is not enough to go around. The judge sees life as a zero-sum game, like poker. There are only so many chips. At the end of the night there are the same number of chips; they have just been redistributed.

When we are conscious we realize the very opposite is true—that we live in a world of abundance. This applies in relationships more than anywhere. We seek relationships to get our connection hopes met. There is an abundance of hopes to go around, an infinite supply. The more love we give, the more there is. Making the choice to extend love to another person in any given moment is how love is created. It is the only way and it always works.

In some areas Kelly and Suzanne were intractable. For example, when Kelly wanted to watch football, Suzanne wanted to throw the set out the window. When Suzanne attended her weekly women's group, Kelly wanted her to have dinner with him at home. They came to me ready to split up, hoping for magic. Instead of dissecting their grievances, I asked each of them to list their hopes for the relationship. They each went into a corner and wrote; then they came back and compared lists. They couldn't believe it. The lists were virtually the same.

Suzanne asked Kelly, "Do you really want us to communicate about our hopes and fears?"

"Yes. Do you really think that each of us being free to learn things outside the relationship will enrich our relationship?"

"Yes, of course I do."

They saw they wanted the same things but their judge language was getting in their way. They made a vow that when either of them felt upset with the other, he or she would declare a conscious conversation. They're still together.

Conditional love, "I'll love you if you do what I want," is not love at all; it is manipulation and coercion. There is no need to sacrifice or surrender who we are or what we want in order to find happiness. The opposite is true. We can develop relationships based on freedom and connection instead of bondage and resentment.

The solution is always the same: I connect in order that my hopes and my partner's hopes may be met. And its corollary: No one needs to sacrifice.

One day we were talking in class about how it was that men often communicate differently from women. Elaine said: "Well, women are the primary nurturers and so they're always the ones who talk about feelings. Men just want to talk about what they're doing."

"Not necessarily," replied Rob. "That's not how it is at my house."

"Oh? How is it at your house?" Elaine asked.

"Well, I'm the one who talks to the kids about their friendships with other kids and how they feel when something goes wrong at school. Samantha is at the office all day and spends a lot of nights catching up on paper work."

"Rob," I asked, "can you give me an example of an interaction at your house, with the actual words people used?"

Rob thought a minute and then said, "Yeah, last Sunday. Samantha and I were sitting in the kitchen and little Josh ran in crying. He went right past Samantha to me. I gave him a big hug and asked him what happened."

"I fell down and hurt my knee," he wailed.

"Oh, that must really hurt. Let me clean it off and put a Band-Aid on it."

"Give it a kiss and make it better," Josh said, wiping his tears with a little fist.

"OK." And I did.

Upon hearing this, many class members raised their eyebrows and a few smiled broadly as they looked at Rob. Rob grinned back, his shaved head and heavily muscled shoulders reflecting the overhead lights. Rob has been a stay-at-home dad for the last eight years and he loves it. The kids love it, too.

Fourth False Relationship Assumption: There is an essential difference between men and women.

Some popular communication books maintain that men and women are so different they seem to come from separate planets. While stereotypes are the judge's stock-in-trade, many people find them limiting. Robin, for example, would have to disagree with the stereotype that nurturing is for women. Being in the Mr. Mom role has allowed his natural capacity for loving and nurturing to blossom. And Robin is not a special case. In a landmark study, Dr. Kyle Pruett of Yale University has shown that, when thrust by circumstances into to the role of primary caregiver, virtually all men demonstrate the innate capacity to nurture, just as much as women do.

William Pollack, Ph.D., assistant clinical professor of psychiatry at Harvard Medical School writes: "In recent studies that look at biological (rather than behavioral) markers of empathic response... researchers have found that when responding to the urgent cries of a young infant, there are no differences between how men and women react." Stereotypes are not who we really are. They are judge folklore, which can become self-fulfilling prophecy.

Men and women communicate differently because their judges were trained differently. The way to healing and happy relationships is to recognize the truth of our underlying shared humanity. And the essence of that humanity is the capacity to love.

Solution: Remember that we are essentially the same with the same positive hopes. Men and women are biological equals in the realm of feelings.

Newlywed Charles, a big man with a warm, infectious smile, loved his wife. He was generous, passionate, tender and kind to her, but he had never come right out and said the words "I love you." He knew she wanted to hear them, but he felt acutely embarrassed and afraid to tell her. He'd never said those words in his life and was afraid she might laugh or think less of him.

Our group reassured him. We persuaded Charles to role-play, saying "Eileen, I love you," to 56-year-old Thelma, who cheerfully stood in for Eileen. We encouraged him say the words from his heart, with full eye contact, until everyone felt his sincerity. It took Charles quite a few tries, but finally he said it in a way that convinced everyone in the room.

When Charles came in to the next class he was unable to conceal his huge grin. After feigning reluctance to tell us, we learned that when he told his wife, tears had come to her eyes and she had squeezed him very close. She had been longing to hear him say those words for a long time. Charles beamed triumphantly to our cheers and applause.

Fifth False Relationship Assumption: My partner knows I love him/her.

The solution: Tell your partner.

One Loving Intention

There is only one thought we need to remember in order to have healthy and fulfilling relationships: *I take full responsibility for extending joy in my relationships.* Looking only for the good in your partner is key. A study of couples who have been happily married for over fifty years shows they consistently offer the most charitable interpretations of each other's intentions.

Initiate the positive; giving appreciation is a powerful way of saying, "I love you." When someone meets our hope we feel happy, and verbal appreciation is a way to acknowledge the gift.

Many times sincerely saying "thank you" meets the need. Other times we may want to create mutual joy and improve the quality of connection by expressing our appreciation more clearly. Our motive is to share our happiness about how they have enriched our lives, not to get anything in return or to evaluate them. We say it this way:

"When you made dinner for me"	The action(s) the other has taken. (fact)
"I felt touched and happy"	Our feeling(s)
Because I was really wanting to rest when I got home and I love it when you demonstrate that you care for me.	Our fulfilled hope(s)

Our statement of our fulfilled hope is the phrase that lets our partner fully realize the joy with which we received their gift.

The following story shows the effect a husband's appreciation had on his wife.

Larry and Jo Ann were an ordinary couple. Like any other couple, they struggled to make ends meet and to do the right things for their children. They were ordinary in yet another way—they had their squabbles. Much of their conversation concerned what was wrong in their marriage and who was to blame. Until one day a most extraordinary event took place.

"You know, Jo Ann, I've got a magic set of drawers. Every time I open them, they're full of socks and underwear," Larry said. "I want to thank you for filling them for all these years."

Jo Ann stared at her husband over the top of her glasses. "What do you want, Larry?"

"Nothing. I just want you to know I appreciate those magic drawers."

This wasn't the first time Larry had done something odd, so Jo Ann pushed the incident out of her mind until a few days later.

"Jo Ann, thank you for recording so many correct check numbers in the ledger this month. You put down the right number 15 out of 16 times. That's a record."

Disbelieving what she had heard, Jo Ann looked up from her

mending. "Larry, you're always complaining about my recording the wrong check numbers. Why stop now?"

"No reason. I just wanted you to know I appreciate the effort you're making."

Jo Ann shook her head and went back to mending. "What's got into him?" she thought to herself.

Nevertheless, the next day when Jo Ann wrote a check at the grocery store, she glanced at her checkbook to confirm that she had put down the right check number. "Why do I suddenly care about those dumb check numbers?" she asked herself.

She tried to disregard the incident, but Larry's strange behavior intensified.

"Jo Ann, that was a great dinner," he said one evening. I appreciate all your effort. Why, in the past 15 years I'll bet you've fixed over 14,000 meals for me and the kids."

Then "Gee, Jo Ann, the house looks spiffy. You've really worked hard to get it looking so good." And even, "Thanks, Jo Ann, for just being you. I really enjoy your company."

Jo Ann was growing worried. "Where's the sarcasm, the criticism?" she wondered.

Her fears that something peculiar was happening to her husband were confirmed by 16-year-old Shelly, who complained, "Dad's gone bonkers, Mom. He just told me I looked nice. With all this makeup and these sloppy clothes, he still said it. That's not Dad, Mom. What's wrong with him?"

Whatever was wrong, Larry didn't get over it. Day in and day out he continued focusing on the positive. Over the weeks, Jo Ann grew more accustomed to her mate's unusual behavior and occasionally even gave him a grudging "Thank you." She prided herself on taking it all in stride, until one day something so peculiar happened, she became completely confused:

"I want you to take a break," Larry said. "I am going to do the dishes. So please take your hands off that frying pan and leave the kitchen."

(Long, long pause.) "Thank you, Larry. Thank you very much!"

Jo Ann's step was now a little lighter, her self-confidence higher and once in a while she hummed. She didn't seem to have as many blue moods anymore. "I rather like Larry's new behavior," she thought.

That would be the end of the story except one day another most extraordinary event took place. This time it was Jo Ann who spoke.

"Larry," she said, "I want to thank you for going to work and providing for us for all these years. I don't think I've ever told you how much I appreciate it."

Larry has never revealed the reason for his dramatic change of behavior no matter how hard Jo Ann has pushed for an answer, and so it will likely remain one of life's mysteries. But it's one Jo Ann is thankful to live with.

Freedom

We are completely free. We don't have to do anything we don't want to do. In fact, no one ever does anything they don't choose to do. A simple way to see this is to make a list of things you do because you "have to."

In one of my groups we discussed this. Daniel said he had to eat and I said he didn't. He said "But I'll starve to death if I don't."

"That's right," I said, "You might. But you don't have to eat. You choose to eat because you prefer the consequences of eating to not eating. So you choose to eat." The group saw that this reasoning could apply to any "have to," such as paying taxes and doing the laundry. They learned to phrase hopes positively, for example "I choose to pay taxes because I enjoy my physical freedom," rather than to "avoid going to jail." "I choose to do laundry because I like to wear clean clothes."

When we realize we are choosing to do something, we can also look at why we are choosing to do it. If our goal is inner peace by getting our hopes met, one of which is to experience and extend joy, then we can look at what we are choosing to do in that light. I choose to eat because it gives me the physical energy to extend joy. Negative motivations are the realm of the judge; positive, loving motivations are our true nature.

"But what about abusive relationships?" asked Charlene. "What if you are living with a perpetrator? Or what if you are the only one giving? With some people you can give and give and they just take and take."

There were two ways I could listen to her question. One would focus on responding to her question as an "expert," someone wiser than her. Such an answer would be: "Then get help. If you are wrestling with a situation in which you do not feel psychologically in control, seek appropriate counseling. If you are afraid for your safety and can't get out, call the police." Charlene, of course, already knew this and my advice would be demeaning.

I chose instead to connect with the feeling energy and guess at the hope behind Charlene's words right now. I said "Charlene, when you ask that, are you feeling anxious because you want to know that someone who has less power in a relationship you're thinking about can be safe?"

"I have a friend who goes from one bad, abusive relationship to the next." Charlene replied. "What can she do?"

"When you see this happening to her are you frustrated because you want to be able to help her?"

"Yes, she rebounds out of a bad relationship and then calls me all elated and invites me to meet this wonderful new guy. The last guy I met was a biker with tattoos and no permanent address. He was crashing at her place."

"So you really care about her and feel frightened sometimes when you see who she trusts."

"Yeah, what can I do?"

"I doubt you can change her. I think that we are most helpful to others when we listen and connect rather than judge. If you feel uncomfortable about her behavior then you can tell her that in terms of your feelings and hopes."

"How would I do that?"

"You could say to her, 'When I met your new man I felt scared because I want you to be safe and happy.' What do you think she'd say back?"

She'd probably laugh and say 'Gee, thanks for your concern, Charlene. I like him and I'd like you to trust my decision on this.'"

"And how would you feel hearing that?" I asked.

"That her life is not my responsibility."

"Can you live comfortably with that?"

"I guess so. It helps if I can tell her how I feel without judging her."

Shirley then spoke up and said "You know, it's not my friends that get under my skin. It's my husband. Somehow he can push my buttons like nobody else."

"When does he push them?"

This group had built a lot of trust and Shirley replied "Well, it happened last Sunday morning when I wanted to make love and he didn't."

"How did you feel?"

"Terrible. Completely rejected. Absolutely miserable."

"What were you looking for? I mean the abstract hope, which making love would have been a demonstration of."

"I like the pleasure and I like lying there afterwards feeling blissed out."

"And what connection hope was met?"

"To feel really at peace, like I belong, like I'm loved."

"So what could you say to your husband?"

"Derek, when you said you didn't want to make love, I felt horrible, because I want to experience belonging, connectedness, to know I'm loved. Would you be willing to tell me how you feel when I say that?"

"How do you think he'd respond?"

"He'd probably give me a big hug and say 'Let's plan on it this evening.'" (smile)

"So what's hard about that?"

"What's hard is that I feel so rejected at the time I just can't come back with that."

"So you need to find a way to come back to center?"

"Yeah."

The Judge's Finger is on the Trigger

We expect that our partners will meet all our needs, especially our biggest needs for love, caring, and belonging. But for many of us our partners trigger emotional responses that are way out of proportion to what happened, such as when Derek didn't want to make love with Shirley on Sunday morning. It touched something in Shirley that brought up powerful feelings, probably rooted in her past. Because it is so hard to stop blaming our partners when we have been triggered, we need to deliberately practice conscious override:

Recognize when we are triggered. One of our judge's core beliefs has been stepped on. The strength of our anger, fear or sadness is our best clue.

Stop, breathe and center ourselves. We may need time alone to do this, physically breathing deeply and saying a mantra, such as "Breathing in, I calm my body; breathing out, I smile." In our thoughts we repeat the truth to ourselves "I am OK. I will not die. My partner is innocent." Visually we may imagine light filling us and extending to them.

Set the goal to connect with freedom. "There is nothing to defend against. I choose to see only good in my partner. I choose to connect."

Communicate by listening or speaking. Say something such as, "When you did that I felt very upset because it triggered some strong feelings in me. I need a few minutes to clear my thinking. Would you be willing to talk about it a little later?"

Our judges are infantile, both in their desires and in their blame. They quickly substitute our intimate partners of today for our parents and project all our unfulfilled wants and fears onto them. So our partners' naïve actions can throw us into fits of sadness or anger. Calling these actions our "triggers" is appropriate because they precipitate a disproportionate emotional response in us, as a slight pull on a trigger fires a pistol.

Most of us try to prevent the pain and unpleasantness of being triggered by controlling the actions of our partners so they won't behave in certain ways. This strategy is doomed to failure because the problem is not with our partners but inside us.

Perhaps nothing is more difficult than communicating with our partner when we are triggered. The temptation to go along with our judge seems so clearly justified. I mean, of all people, shouldn't my partner know how I feel about this? Shouldn't they love me enough to behave differently?

The path to unhappiness is judging our partner and trying to get them to change. They resent being judged and actively resist our attempts to change them. What does create change, however, is unconditional positive regard, allowing others to be centered and to grow in the ways they wish.

The path to personal happiness is taking responsibility for causing and handling our feelings. We can practice at anytime, telling ourselves, "I am not a victim; I am strong and free," and doing personal empowerment meditations or exercises to build up our energy. Then we can practice choosing joy for ourselves by getting our hopes met through conscious communication.

Love is relational. Love is accepting and freeing, not coercing. Intimate relationships present us with amazing opportunities to practice trust, to disclose fears and disappointments, to confront, to listen without trying to fix, to ask for what we want, and to forgive. Love is a choice to see the light in our partner rather than the shade, and when we choose to see it, there it is.

It's not enough to study them like beetles under a microscope;
you need to know what it feels like to be a beetle.

– ROGER FISHER & WILLIAM URY

CHAPTER TEN

Connecting with Teenagers

While we may be willing to give our intimate partner the benefit of the doubt, we are less likely to be so generous with a teenager. Let's begin by looking at a common judge assumption about teenagers. It goes like this: because teenagers' moral development is incomplete, they are irresponsible and *so we must coerce them* in ways in which we would not coerce an adult. With this assumption as an excuse, our judges take license to judge and pressure teenagers.

Ages 13-19 are developmentally a time of transition from parental control to personal responsibility and freedom. But teens are people who want to get their hopes met in life. How do we want them to accomplish this? Do we want them to be aggressively competitive and lonely or do we want them to connect, form healthy relationships and find inner peace?

The aliveness of teens can embarrass us. If I begin to lecture them they bring life to the situation by fooling around. Teens have highly sensitized "bullshit" detectors. They instantly detect negative judgments and rules that apply to them but not to adults. We are uncomfortable in their presence because they are often less than tactful in bringing these things, and their judgments of us, to our attention. Their judges are still clumsy, not having learned to hide behind more sophisticated language.

On the plus side, teens are highly responsive to personal sharing of feelings and hopes. One day Sara was interrupting constantly and sabotaging my communication class for teens. I got so upset I spoke from my heart: "Sara, I'm frustrated! I'm trying to share something with you that I think is important and I want to be respected. Will you please listen?" Sara turned toward me and looked right at me.

Here's another example. Mark was telling the guys about how he had beaten up his younger brother, totally ignoring my efforts to teach. I turned and said to Mark: "I feel sad about how you beat up your younger brother, because I got a lot from my brother. I want you to hear what I have to say about my brother. My brother taught me to play chess and to ride a motorcycle." Mark's head turned and he brushed the flag of dirty blond hair from his eyes.

Our Two Options

When faced with motivating a reluctant teenager, it is good for us to remember that we have power over them. This presents us with an important choice. Our first option: *We can motivate them to do what we want out of fear because we are the authority; we can coerce them.* In this case they may well resist, try to get out of doing it, or later try to get back at us. We are dealing with them on the judge level. When coerced to do what we want, they may do it this time but are unlikely to do it on their own in the future.

I could have told Sara, "Be quiet or else I'll have you expelled from the youth center." I could have told Mark to stop gloating about beating his brother because that was a childish way to behave and that he was a coward to pick on someone smaller than he was. Such comments would have made me a punisher and the kids would not have continued to come to my voluntary program.

Our other option is to *afford teens respect and use conscious communication to motivate them through positive attraction, having them do what we would like because they see how it helps us get our hopes met.* This is personal rather than authoritative. In the process, they experience getting their own hope to help others met. This hope is a powerful force in them. When fulfilled, it gives them the experience of really making a difference in someone else's life, enhancing their self-esteem. They realize they matter.

Motivating by coercion and motivating by positive attraction both work in the short run. But only one works over time and builds character. We can project our judge's fears onto teenagers and treat them critically, but they only learn to condemn others and themselves. Or we can choose to view them compassionately, treating them with encouragement and approval so they learn confidence and to appreciate others as well as themselves.

I have taught conscious communication to many "at risk" teenagers. They recognize its value in improving relationships just as adults do. One of teenagers' biggest needs is to learn how to express their feelings and hopes in conflict situations without becoming verbally aggressive or physically violent.

Cherie and Anita were friends, but of late the friendship had been rocky. One day Anita took Cherie's jacket out of her locker and wore it. Cherie's first reaction was to blast Anita "You are totally rude. Don't you ever touch anything of mine again! " Fast as lightning, Anita attacked Cherie right back. After we centered ourselves and discussed it in the group, Cherie rephrased her communication this way:

"Anita,"	Opener
"When you took my jacket out of my locker and wore it without asking me	Fact
"I felt upset	Feeling
"because I want my privacy and my things to be respected.	Hope
"Would you be willing to ask me next time you want something of mine?"	Request

Anita immediately responded "Yes, but you know what really makes me angry is when I tell you something that's a secret and then you tease me about it in front of other people."

"Well, you just tease me right back; I didn't think it bothered you."

"Yeah, well it hurts."

"Ya know, it hurts when you tease me too."

Having opened the door to honest feeling exchange they jumped right in, talked it out, and came up with agreements that re-solidified their friendship. At the end of class, they were sitting on the same couch, grinning as they shared a walkman headset.

Once teenagers have learned conscious communication, they often transfer the skills to other contexts in their own lives.

Tiffany was a powerful eighth grader, both physically and personally. She was intelligent, a natural leader and had a group of a dozen junior high outcasts who followed her. Violent solutions to conflicts with other kids were frequent. They stuck together to protect each other. Tiffany didn't hesitate to verbally attack teachers in front of the class. While her accusations about injustices were accurate, her manner of speaking drove adults to heights of anger they hadn't previously known they could reach.

Then Tiffany took the conscious communication program. Toward the end of program, she reported one of the boys in her group to school authorities for having drugs and a knife in his locker. Before doing so, she obtained a promise from the school authorities that they wouldn't take action against the boy. The authorities promptly broke their promise to her and suspended him. The boy told Tiffany she was a traitor and he'd never speak to her again.

Using her new communication skills, she told him "I did it because I really care about you and I was afraid for your safety."

Then, Tiffany met with, and obtained an apology from, the school authorities for breaking their promise. In a program evaluation a few weeks later, her principal wrote, "Tiffany has gone from being very confrontational to very appropriate." She not only won the respect of the adults; the boy who was suspended became her boyfriend.

Boys have a noticeably harder time transferring conscious communication to life situations than girls do. Girls understand and apply them almost immediately. Boys understand just as quickly, but, because of their masculine conditioning, resist applying them in their personal lives.

This was illustrated just after the "final exam" of a class of boys with whom I had been working for a year. They had passed the exam and solidly understood the concepts of conscious communication. I was proud of them as I left to pick up the celebratory pizzas down the street.

When I came back they were in an uproar. Someone had destroyed a sweater belonging to Nathan's sister and red-faced Nathan was halfway out the door, on his way to beat the pulp out of a suspect. The other boys were cheering him on. Although his sister said all she wanted was a new sweater, it took over half an hour to bring Nathan back to center.

As we know, boys learn to be tough and hide all their feelings except anger. What can we do about it? Clinical psychologist William Pollack, founding member and Fellow of the Society for the Psychological Study of Men and Masculinity, writes: "Above all, we can begin to teach connection as the basis of a new male model."

His recommendations for helping boys reconnect include:

1. Look behind their anger for more vulnerable feelings.

2. Encourage boys to express their sadness and fear.

3. Let them know they don't have to be strong or "act like a man."

4. Do not tease or shame them.

When I was in school I gave and received a lot of sarcasm, teasing, and "zingers." This is not to be dismissed as OK, boys-will-be-boys stuff. It is harmful and we have a responsibility to model and to teach a more positive way of communicating.

In the social and emotional learning program that I teach for "at risk" teens, Justin was a major challenge. Towering over me, he frequently interrupted to shift the conversation to violent topics or to describe how he had intimidated other teachers. Though only 15, he had already been jailed for assault and had impregnated his girlfriend.

In the program, Justin was slowly able to touch his emotional self. As he became honest with me, a mutual trust developed. He told how his drug-pusher father had only a fleeting relationship with his mother. The only time his mother spoke to Justin, other than to yell at him, was to bum cigarettes late at night when she was stoned. Justin learned important skills in the group, such as how to talk his way out of potential fights and how to speak to authority figures without vulgar language. He was delighted as he began to avoid the familiar penalties at school. Later, Justin remarked, apparently off-handedly, "That program saved my life."

Demonstrating Connection

The teenagers I work with appreciate seeing methods of conflict resolution acted out physically. Aikido, a martial art with the goal of restoring harmony rather than defeating an opponent, provides vivid physical demonstrations of conscious communication.

The key principles of aikido are: get out of the way, connect, and hold the other person until they return to center. Attacks are considered as gifts of energy to be used creatively and harmoniously.

Tom Crum, aikido master and author, writes: "The martial art of aikido offers a useful metaphor for shifting our way of thinking and acting in conflict situations. Using aikido, we are able to experience the resolution of physical conflicts, actual bodily attacks, without the use of unnecessary force. Attacks are neutralized without injury. Life is protected and nurtured. When we experience this unique approach on a physical level, we are more able to let go of solidified beliefs and inappropriate patterns in the rest of our lives."

How can we as parents help our teenagers if we can't send them to a conscious communication or an aikido program? We simply practice conscious communication with them. For example, Seth's mother was concerned about her son's bad attitude about school. The dialog below shows how she would have talked with him prior to learning conscious listening.

Seth, throwing down his books, said loudly, "School sucks."

"That's no way to talk," she quickly corrected.

"I hate school."

"I felt that way when I was your age," his mother replied, "but later on I saw the importance of a good education. Stick with it and you'll see."

"Why stick with something useless? What good are polynomials going to do me as a waiter?"

"A waiter? Is this a joke?"

"Oh yeah! Brian quit school and is making good money as a waiter."

"You don't want to be a waiter. You can do better than that. If you stay in school and get a good education you can get a much better job."

"Brian's got his own place and a car."

"Seth, here you are, wanting to quit school when you haven't really tried. You have so much potential."

"Come on, Mom. I've been trying at school for years. It's just a waste of time. It isn't worth it. I'm sick of it."

"You can't quit now, after coming so far. If you'd just sit down every afternoon and do your homework instead of flipping on the TV..."

"Just forget it Mom. I don't want to talk about it."

In this example, Seth's mother was trying to address her own concerns about Seth before listening to him. She tragically cut off her opportunity to help him. People in pain do not welcome our telling them that they are wrong and need to be fixed. They want compassion, connection, and understanding.

Let's see how this scenario might change if Seth's mom practiced conscious communication. The conscious communication elements are presented on the right.

"School sucks."

"You sound pretty upset about school."   Feeling guess

"I am. It's a waste of time. I don't get
anything useful out of it."

"So you're upset because you want   Feeling guess
something useful?"   Hope guess

"Yes. I want to be a waiter. Brian quit
school. He's a waiter and making a lot
of money."

"So you like what Brian is doing."   Paraphrase

"Yeah, at least he's not wasting time for
no reason. He's successful."

"Are you bored and wanting to be successful?"	Feeling guess Hope guess
"Yes, and I'm sure as hell wasting my time in algebra."	
"Tell me more."	Prompt
"Mom, I just can't seem to get it. I studied for hours for the last test and I failed it."	
"That does sound frustrating."	Feeling guess
"I hate it. I don't want to take it!"	
"You really don't want to take algebra."	Paraphrase
"Yeah, Mom. What can I do?"	Connection established, energy shift
"I'm concerned and would like to be helpful. Is there anything I can do?"	expresses own feeling and hope
"I don't know."	
"How about if I talk to your teacher, see what she says?"	guesses at request
"Maybe."	begin joint problem-solving

Seth's mother has come a long way in her in her ability to listen and to connect with Seth. The chance of their working out a mutually acceptable solution now looks pretty good.

Teenagers' emotional upset often shows up in annoying behavior that we can learn to see for what it is, a call for help. The Johnson family was in crisis when they came to me for family mediation. Because of their work schedules Mom, Dad, and Tim had been coming and going in the house at different hours, almost never seeing each other.

But now Tim, at fifteen, was breaking rules at home and getting into trouble at school, frequently arriving late and sometimes not at all. Tim stated in the first session that he "couldn't stand" living at home and was going to move out and live with a friend.

During a few mediation sessions I taught the family how to listen to one another and how to express their feelings. During the final mediation session Mom promised to stop being a nag, if Tim would promise to take responsibility for getting to school on time. Agreed. They planned to have certain meals together. Then Dad said, "Tim, I love you and respect you. I'd like to help you fix up the truck." A dam was broken.

"I thought you just didn't care about me," Tim sobbed, giving voice to the reason he couldn't stand living at home. At the close of the session, they were crying and hugging each other. I will always be grateful to have witnessed this moment of connection. It takes courage to expose one's heart, and often teenagers show that courage more readily than adults do.

My goal in life is to unite my avocation with my vocation
As my two eyes make one sight.
For only where love and need are one
And work is play for mortal stakes
Is the deed ever really done
For heaven's and for future's sake.

– ROBERT FROST

CHAPTER ELEVEN

Being Influential at Work

Have you ever heard a person say, "I hate my job, but I need the money." Or "Don't get your hopes up about your fun idea; management only cares about the bottom line." Or "Don't let the boss catch you doing that." They all have one thing in common, the attitude of the person saying them.

The judge's attitude toward work is, *I have to do meaningless work or I'll starve.* Clearly, this attitude is based on scarcity and also on the idea that we are separate from and in competition with other people. We buy into this attitude whenever we think we have to sacrifice control of ourselves, that we have to do things we don't really want to do and that we can't express the caring, relational part of ourselves at work.

Our thinking, generated from this attitude, is the source of our stress and suffering. We are seeing ourselves as helpless victims. And our unconscious attitudes will continue to control us until we become aware of them and choose differently. The stakes here are big, because we spend most of our lives at work.

Part of the problem has been our excessive focus on money because, as a medium of exchange, it only works on the physical level. To use money in place of personally expressing appreciation diminishes both of us. We have missed an emotional connection. While financial rewards meet physical needs, they are not food for our heart or spirit, and as relational beings we suffer on a diet of money at the expense of connection. When we focus on something higher—peace of mind and getting hopes met—money reverts to its rightful place, a lightly held preference.

Dick Leader conducted more than 1,000 interviews with people who retired from leading companies after lucrative, distinguished careers. They said that if they could live their lives over again they would do things outside of their own financial self-interest, things that contribute to life, that add value to others, because these are what bring personal fulfillment. They also said they would be more courageous in relationships.

Finding Meaning in Our Work

We can find fulfillment and joy at work by seeing it as *an opportunity to give.* First, we work to help others get their physical needs met, but more importantly, *on the conscious level, we work to help people get their hopes met as well as to get our hopes met.* Seeing it this way we take responsibility for our lives at work.

Many have found that *viewing work as service to others* transforms work from drudgery to joy. Albert Schweitzer said, "The only ones among you who will be truly happy are those who have sought and found how to serve." We can choose to focus on making a difference in the lives of others. Why not now? Whatever we do for work, we can view our daily interactions as helping other people.

And we will be richly rewarded, because the most challenging and important hopes for people to experience at work are respect and appreciation.

Creating Respect

Roger, an apprentice fireman, was the victim of cruel hazing from senior firefighters. Roger came into our group very upset one evening after a particularly humiliating incident in which a senior firefighter lied to him. He was ready to quit. In the group, we talked about what the senior firefighter might have been thinking and feeling. Our group role-played a way that Roger might handle it.

The next week Roger reported that he had confronted the man and, although he departed from his "script," he had stuck to the spirit of true empathy. He stated his piece but deliberately refrained from verbally attacking the other man. Roger said the firefighter changed completely. After their confrontation he spent several hours of his own time showing Roger what he really needed to know about the fire equipment so he could win the respect of the other men. Roger had gained a mentor, and he stayed with the fire department.

For a closer look at the process of creating respect, here is a brief dialogue between a sales manager and a salesperson. Imagine you are the salesperson. You had a verbal agreement with a customer, but the deal fell through. You have just informed your manager that the customer backed out and your manager says: "That was dumb not to use the forms and get it in writing."

Here are three different ways in which you could respond:

Judge the manager: "You always criticize me before you know the details." This is not respectful of the manager.

Judge yourself: "Yeah, maybe I'm not up to this." This is not respectful of yourself.

Connect: "Are you concerned because you want your salespeople to make solid contracts?"

This last response respectfully guesses at the manager's hope. Connecting with the manager does not weaken your position. Although it may require a few guesses, when complete it allows the manager to experience being fully understood and to return to center. It shows you both that the manager's intention was not to attack.

Then you, as the salesperson, are in a strong position to state your own feeling and hope. For example you might say "Yes, I'm upset because I was really hoping to make that sale," validating the manger's concern, and then adding either your explanation of what happened or requesting help, whatever is true and appropriate for you. Choosing to look for the manager's positive intention honors our mutual hope for respect.

In my experience, managers know that people make mistakes and that unplanned events occur. They are impressed with people who learn from these situations rather than defend themselves. On a broader level people are more impressed with who we really are than with our judges.

In the work environment we do sometimes modify our communication slightly from the way we say things at home. In the last example, use of the mild feeling word "concerned" is appropriate because the manager is more likely to acknowledge it than he would the word "afraid." Of the two conscious communication elements, feeling and hope, accurately identifying the hope is more important for connection than identifying the exact feeling.

Managing People

Now let's look, from a manager's shoes, at how to respectfully manage people. The judge attitude about managing is that lazy or irresponsible workers must be coerced to do what they're supposed to do. Here is how that attitude played out for Stuart:

Stuart was a shipping supervisor for a large manufacturer of stereo speakers. His boss called him into his office and, with considerable annoyance, told him, "Two customers called this week and complained that they damaged their speakers cutting open the boxes. I traced both shipments to your shift. Find the problem and straighten it out right away." Stuart went to the shipping area and noticed that Jeff was not putting in one of the usual pieces of cardboard as he packed speakers.

Typical (Judge) Work Scenario

"Hey, Jeff, what are you doing?"

"Packing speaker boxes."

"Why aren't you putting this piece of cardboard in here? Don't you remember, I just trained you two weeks ago?"

"Yeah, I remember."

"Well, then do it. I just got chewed out by the boss because two customers damaged their speakers unpacking them."

"Well, that's not my fault. How can I control how they unpack them? Do you expect me to ride along with each shipment and say 'Now be very careful unpacking these?'"

"I'm getting really tired of your sarcastic attitude, Jeff. Do you want to pack the boxes like you're supposed to or do you want to walk?"

"I'll pack 'em."

"Good, and please re-pack any boxes of yours that haven't left the dock."

"Okay."

We can sense that Jeff had an adverse reaction to Stuart's words. When Stuart left Jeff might well have been thinking, *If I can find a way to make you or the company pay for coercing me, I'll do it.* Is Jeff a bad person or could Stuart have made some communication mistakes?

Explanation of Stuart's Mistakes

Stuart	Type of Mistake
	No "opener."
"Hey, Jeff, what are you doing?"	Questioning—shows that analysis and judgment are coming.
"Why aren't you putting this piece of cardboard in here?	Questioning.
Don't you remember, I just trained you two weeks ago?"	Blame in question form
	Not listening to Jeff's side.
"Well, then do it."	Demand—has threat behind it.
"I just got chewed out by the boss because two customers damaged their speakers unpacking them."	Not taking responsibility.
"I'm getting tired of your sarcastic attitude."	Attacking, judging
"Do you want to pack the boxes like you're supposed to or do you want to walk?"	Ultimate threat in question form.
"Good, and please re-pack any boxes of yours that haven't left the dock."	Demand.

Stuart's judge brought out a defensive response in Jeff. We, however, know that people are essentially good, and when they don't do what they're supposed to do, they have a reason. A fifteen-year study revealed the primary reasons for poor performance. Here are two of the most common:

1. Workers don't know what they are supposed to do, or why they should do it, or how to do it.

    This is generally because they were not fully informed about the task and how it fits into the whole job.

    Solution: Respectfully tell them using an appropriate opener, fact, feeling, hope, and request.

2. Workers think the manager's way of doing the task won't work or that their way is better.

    Solution: Ask their opinion. Guess at their feelings and hopes. When they've been heard, share yours. Then make requests until you find agreement.

Now let's see how Stuart could have handled the situation more respectfully, using conscious communication.

Same Scenario with Conscious Communication

Stuart (S) and Jeff (J)	Jeff's Thoughts
S: "Hi Jeff, I want your help in finding a way to resolve a customer satisfaction problem.	*He needs my help. The problem is about the customer, not me.*
Do you have a minute to talk about it now?"	*I have time.*
J: "Sure."	*I wonder what it's about?*

S: "The boss just told me that two customers damaged their speakers while unpacking them."

There are clumsy people in the world.

"I'm concerned because I think it may have to do with packing. I noticed you didn't put this piece of cardboard in the box you just packed."

That's right.

"Will you share your thinking?"

Delighted to tell you.

J: "Yeah, that would be a waste of packing material. See, look at this, the way I do it these corner pieces lock the speakers in so they can't bounce around."

I should get credit for saving the company material (which costs money) and for not adding more unnecessary trash to the environment.

S: "So you've found a more efficient way to pack the speakers?"

Pretty close, I think he's about to see it.

J: "Yes, the speakers are safe and it saves packing material."

Now he should get it all

S: "I see why you leave it out. Now would you be willing to hear what I'm thinking about it?"

Sure, since you can see the advantages of how I'm doing it.

J: "Okay."

S: "Many customers cut the boxes open with a knife along this line where the tape is. That piece of cardboard fits right under the line and keeps their knife from hitting the speaker."

Oops, I hadn't thought of that. Why don't the customers think for a second?

J: "Oh, why don't we just put a picture of a huge knife with a red x over it on the box to warn them?"

S: "We tried that and some customers cut the speakers anyway."	*Dumb customers.*

J: "How stupid can you get?"

S: "Are you annoyed about having to put in the extra piece?"	*Yes, and embarrassed that I didn't know this. It makes sense to me now.*
J: "Yes, but given the possibility of damaging the speakers, we better put it in."	*I'm no dummy. I'll show him I understand that using the extra resources is necessary.*

We can see that Stuart's new communication brought forth a much better response in Jeff. Here's how he did it.

Explanation of Stuart's Conscious Communication

Stuart	Type of Conscious Communication
S: "Hi Jeff, I want your help in finding a way to resolve a customer satisfaction problem."	Positive "opener" shows supervisor's hope
"Do you have a minute to talk about it now?"	Respectful request.
S: "The boss just told me that two customers damaged their speakers while unpacking them."	Fact.

"I'm concerned	
because I	Feeling.
think it may have to do with packing.	Taking responsibility for feeling.
I noticed you didn't put this piece of cardboard in the box you just packed."	Fact.
"Will you share your thinking?"	
S: "So you've found a more efficient way to pack the speakers?"	Requests Jeff's side of it. Guesses at hope
S: "I see why you leave it out.	
Now would you be willing to hear what I'm thinking about it?"	Confirms understanding. Requests opportunity to express own point of view.
S: "Many customers open the boxes with a knife along this line where the tape is. That piece of cardboard fits right under the line and keeps their knife from hitting the speaker."	Fact.
S: "We tried that and some customers cut the speakers anyway."	Fact.
S: "Are you annoyed about having to put in the extra piece?"	Guesses at feeling. Guesses at hope.

Jeff volunteered to put in the extra
piece of cardboard, otherwise
Stuart would have made a   Request.

We can see the benefits of speaking respectfully to Jeff. He had thought that his way of packing the boxes was better. When given true empathy by his supervisor, he was quite willing to add the piece of cardboard. He might even sell his coworkers on the idea.

The importance of conscious communication at work can not be over-emphasized. Let Davidson, Ph.D., in his recent book, *Wisdom At Work: The Awakening of Consciousness in the Workplace*, writes "... skillful interpersonal relationships and open communication, including the free flow of constructive and positive feedback, not only enhance business performance and teamwork but generate intangible morale as well."

Improved ability to communicate brings benefits on broader levels, such as between companies. A project team at a multi-national integrated-circuit chip manufacturer had failed in its mission to improve delivery response time to a major customer corporation. The team had collapsed and blamed its failure on management's lack of support.

I regrouped the team and taught them how to listen to others and speak more directly. They then confronted the managers who had let them down and created a new team charter. They negotiated directly with their contacts in the customer corporation, defining their specific needs, and found ways to dramatically improve their company's response time. They became corporate heroes and a full page portrait of the leader of the team was printer on the cover of the company's worldwide magazine.

Leadership

Each of us can be a leader, a person who lives consciously and sets an example. To quote Albert Schweitzer: "Example is not the main thing in influencing others, it is the only thing." People are motivated by attraction.

Leaders are self-aware. They know how to find peace and joy in themselves, and this allows them to see it in others and the world. When we do this we are putting into practice ancient wisdom: "We do not see things as they are. We see them as we are," (the Talmud). Leaders are those who assume abundance rather than scarcity. This allows them to be detached from the small stuff and to model integrity and humility. Great leaders listen to others and accept feedback; they freely admit mistakes.

To be a leader means expressing our caring for others. While it takes courage to do this in the workplace, the benefits are extraordinary. Herb Kelleher, president of Southwest Airlines, expresses his care for his employees in many ways, such as by giving out Heroes of the Heart awards. His airline has won the "triple crown" for passenger service (best on-time performance, fewest bags lost, and least passenger complaints) nine times. No competitor has ever achieved that. This attitude toward people has also translated into financial gain. Southwest was the top performing stock from 1972 to 1992, with a 21,775% return!

Love is the missing power in the workplace. Let Davidson writes, "As the emotional basis for empowerment and partnership efforts, love means believing in people and holding them as able. This often requires the x-ray vision to see through people's reservations about their limitations to the deeper promise." This is exactly what we do when we use conscious communication to center others and to tap into their hopes.

A few years ago I was called into a company in the throes of a major crisis. The staff and managers complained vociferously about each other. Staff members refused to cooperate with one another and only covered for themselves. The working environment was antagonistic and tense. The quality of service had declined precipitously, leaving many customers seriously dissatisfied; some even filed complaints with government agencies. The company found itself near the brink of disaster.

After training the managers and staff in conscious communication, I directed them to talk with each other, first while I observed their technique in small groups, then in independent pairs to resolve specific issues. To everyone's relief genuine cooperation was established between individuals who had previously expressed great animosity. Two departments with long histories of blaming and sniping at each other learned to support one another. Customers noticed the difference and the complaints stopped. As the staff found they had created a pleasant place to work, turnover lessened.

Learning to take responsibility for their thoughts and to communicate respectfully, each had become a leader.

There is no act, large or small, fine or mean, which springs from any motive but the one—the necessity of appeasing and contenting one's own spirit..

– MARK TWAIN

CHAPTER TWELVE

Conversing with Your Judge

Early one Saturday morning, Elizabeth's tossing and turning in bed awoke me. It was still dark and I was irritated. *Damn it*, I thought. *I went to bed late; my head feels like a sludge bucket. If I wake up now I'll be miserable all day from lack of sleep.* Then I realized I was about to begin the day on an angry note. I remembered that only my thoughts could be the cause of my irritation. Nonetheless, a quick debate went on in my head: *No, Elizabeth is making me angry. No, my thoughts are.*

I finally chose conscious override and said to myself: "I'm OK; only my thoughts are making me upset. Elizabeth is innocent. She's probably feeling anxious and wanting comfort." I put my arms around her.

The next thing I knew, the sun was streaming in the window. We both woke up smiling. I had appeased and contented my own spirit by choosing to change my thinking. It was an act of self-love. And it worked out pretty well for Elizabeth, too.

If our choice is to live in happiness, self-love is the place to begin. The judge's path is habitual, but if happiness is our goal, the other path is easier than we think. Because when we choose joy instead of fear, *we have an invincible friend, love, working with us.*

About the healing power of self-love, Bernie Siegel, M.D., said, "I am convinced that unconditional love is the most powerful known stimulant of the immune system. If I told patients to raise their blood levels of immune globulins or killer T cells, no one would know how. But if I can teach them to love themselves and others fully, the same changes happen automatically. The truth is: love heals."

Ten years ago I would not have chosen to put my arms around a restless Elizabeth. For the first forty years of my life I had tried to be a loving person and had failed. What motivated me to find, develop and use conscious communication? A desire, born of desperation, to change myself. When I divorced I hit the bottom of the self-image barrel. I ceaselessly told myself "You're a loser," "You're a piece of ...." "Killing yourself is the only honorable way out." But killing myself would not have raised other people's views of me, would not have helped me and would have been a terrible blow to my son.

I chose to live and to do my best to make a better life for him. To do this, I needed to become a better person. I threw myself into recovery from addictive thinking, began psychotherapy, and pursued spiritual growth with determination. After several months I realized that my low self-image had been incorrect. I learned that I was good and much the same as other people. I had been a good person all along. I began to like and eventually to love myself. I was now telling myself "You are good, kind, strong, healthy, loving and lovable." I found the tools I needed to improve my life and my life changed. The twelve-step support group techniques and psychotherapy were readily available when I chose to look for them. But I was luckier in finding the communication tools, and gratefully dedicated myself to sharing them with others.

The Importance of Our Self-Image

We are not born with a self-image. As we grow our self-image develops, first as a result of how our parents and other people judge us. We believe we are as they see us. As we get older we compare ourselves with others to see if we are better or worse in looks, talent, and popularity. In so doing we solidify our self-image. From then on, psychologists have discovered, we seek to confirm that self-image, not to change it. People with high esteem seek out people who confirm their positive self-image. People with low esteem do the reverse. Reluctant to challenge or to change the self-image we have been given, it is easy to remain stuck with our sad view of ourselves.

Here are two examples that illustrate how self-image influences our response to positive and to negative events.

Melissa thought of herself as inept and unlovable. One day she received a love note from a young man she'd recently met and her first reaction was to think the message couldn't true, that it was a joke. After rereading it many times, she decided he was sincere. But then she thought about what she knew about him and found flaws in him. The next day she thought it possible that the note was true and the sender worthy, but then she feared that something would mess it up, and that her unworthiness would be discovered.

By the time she was ready to respond, she learned he had moved on.

Janice, on the other hand, really liked herself. She got an anonymous obscene phone call on her answering machine and dismissed it as stupid. The phone rang again while she was at home; she picked it up and it was the guy who'd left the message.

She laughed and said, "Well, that was an unusual way to introduce yourself. Sounds like you'd like someone to talk to." There followed a pause and Janice added. "So my name's Janice. Would you like to talk a while?"

After another pause she heard, "OK." So she continued to talk, guessing tactfully at his unmet hopes for connection and acceptance. She learned a few things about him. At the end of the conversation he said, "Hey, thanks for talking."

Janice's response was exceptional because our judges believe strongly in enemies. Janice overrode that thought. The belief in defending ourselves against enemies is founded in fear and it generates more fear, because we fear whatever we defend against or attack. To see innocence puts us in a stronger position. If people are essentially good there is nothing to attack us.

Our self-image is our biggest self-fulfilling prophecy. Research proves that people who see themselves as incompetent sabotage their relationships and don't pursue new, positive relationships. People who expect to be rejected see themselves as rejected where others have not intended to reject them.

In addition to people reacting to our tone and facial expression, our emotional energy also resonates *invisibly* with other people. As a tuning fork, vibrating at middle C and held over a piano, will cause the middle C string to vibrate, we create a field of energy around us. This energy field harmonizes with what is similar to it. If we are fearful, fearful people and events appear in our lives.

Having a low self-image is tragic because it is based on error. Our judge believed the negativity other people had about us when we were too young to know differently. The tragedy is that we recreate and perpetuate their false assumptions about us in the present.

The self-image formation process takes place in our heads. And from this strategic location, we can begin to change the one relationship that determines the nature of all our relationships—our relationship with ourselves.

We will be able to practice conscious communication more successfully when we have a positive self-image. Here is a practical, three-fold approach:

1. Changing our beliefs about ourselves

2. Getting to know our conscious selves

3. Dialogging with our judge voices

Let's look at each in turn.

Changing Our Beliefs About Ourselves

Many of us are self-critical, at least part of the time. In certain situations, we put ourselves down by saying to ourselves such things as "I can't do that. I'll fail" and statements such as:

"I'm weak."

"I'm afraid."

"I must be perfect."

"I'll be rejected."

"I'm guilty."

Notice that we get a certain psychological payoff with these statements. We get to remain safe within our familiar boundaries. Our judge sets up these limits in an attempt to protect us, to keep us from taking risks. He is well intentioned! His statements to us have protective beliefs behind them.

Judge's statement	Judge's belief
"I'm weak."	Don't put yourself in a position where you might get hurt.
"I'm afraid."	Watch out for people who might attack you.
"I must be perfect."	Don't make a mistake or you'll be punished.

| "I'll be rejected." | Don't take the risk of being vulnerable. |
| "I'm guilty." | If I've been judged as bad, maybe I can mitigate some of the punishment by punishing myself. |

The judge's beliefs boil down to "I don't want you to get hurt." The trouble with them is that they box us in. As we become aware of our judge's negative beliefs, we can change our limiting self-talk. Our conscious intention is a powerful creative force. It can free us.

So we don't attack our well-intentioned judge. Instead we say "no" to him in the same respectful way that we already know, by validating his hope. Imagine you are invited to go mountain climbing and a voice in your head speaks right up, "You could get seriously hurt or lost up there. Don't go."

You find yourself partly excited and wanting to go but partly anxious and worried.

You could consciously reply to the voice in your head, "Thank you for your concern about my safety." And then share your hope, "My hope is to grow personally, to enjoy the companionship of my friends and the beauty of the mountain."

Then you check in with your judge, "How do you feel when you hear that?" And then dialog with him.

Judge: "I'm afraid you'll sprain your ankle."

"You're really worried I'll hurt myself?"

"Yes."

"Now I see the reason for your hesitation. Would you like some assurance that I'll be safe?"

"Yes, and that you'll bring rain gear."

"I have good equipment; I'll follow all the procedures for mountain safety, my friends will be there and I'll be careful. Are you convinced?"

"Oh, OK. But be careful."

Then you notice that your hesitation is gone. Your fearful voice has been reassured by being fully heard. You can write down dialogs like this for yourself so they are even more powerful.

We have an even greater opportunity—to establish new beliefs about ourselves by using affirmations. We can begin to build a stronger self-image so that we have more rapid and positive influence over our fearful voices. We can live in greater conscious harmony with our judge.

Affirmative self-talk establishes our new beliefs firmly in our minds. We simply write down and repeat the positive opposite of our fearful internal messages. When phrasing our affirmations we are careful to state what we do want, not what we don't want, using the present tense without qualifiers. For example, instead of saying "I'll try to stop being late," we would say "I arrive at the right time."

Judge's statement	Our loving affirmation
"I'm weak."	"I'm strong."
"I'm afraid."	"I'm confident."
"I must be perfect."	"I'm fine as I am."
"I'll be rejected."	"I'm accepted."
"I'm guilty."	"I'm innocent. I am well intentioned. Making a mistake is human and forgivable."

We may not believe our affirmations at first, but practice is the key to fulfillment. Repetition creates belief. As we focus on our new self-image, we create it. We can dwell on our fears, based on a choice made long ago, or we can focus on our hopes and bring joy into our lives.

There are many ways to practice positive self-talk: posting our affirmations, carrying them with us on cards, making an audio-tape, talking about them in support groups. The key is to repeat them often. Here is a reminder of how our belief changes our world.

Our belief in our new self-image influences our

⇩

Choice of which thoughts we entertain

⇩

Our thoughts and feelings create

⇩

Our Psychological Reality

Changing our beliefs about ourselves is a broad project. We start one step at a time. Through practice we can gently change our long-term image of ourselves.

Getting to Know Our Conscious Selves

Our thinking is completely under our conscious control. It's like our breathing, which goes on all the time without our awareness, but we can hold our breath or change its pace anytime we want to. We can become aware of and change our thinking. If you set your mind to think something, there is nothing anyone can do to make you change your mind. Yet you can change it in an instant, anytime you want to.

Our judge, or unconscious mind, dwells in the body, in the realm of our senses, where it generates 99% of our thoughts. To experience our conscious mind, we still our physical senses. We can think of it either as transcending the body or going deeper than the body.

The practice of quiet wakefulness is meditation. In meditation we come to appreciate the unimportance of most of our thoughts as they go by. We become aware of our true peaceful nature. Meditation dissolves stress. There are many schools of meditation. We can choose a path that speaks to us, that brings us peace. Here is one way to meditate.

How to meditate

1. Sit comfortably, close your eyes and relax.

2. Breathe through your nose; notice the cool in-breath in your nostrils.

3. Silently to yourself, begin repeating a word or phrase of your choosing such as: love, om, peace, in/out or let it be.

4. Each time you realize that you have been distracted by thoughts, feelings, or noises, gently bring your attention back to repeating your word or phrase.

5. Continue for ten to twenty minutes.

6. Sit quietly for a minute or so afterwards, allowing other thoughts to return. Slowly open your eyes and sit for another minute. Don't judge your experience, regardless of whether you have had many thoughts or just a few.

There are two things we may notice. First we may notice the nature of our feelings (bored, anxious) and of our thoughts (remembering, analyzing, imagining). As we become aware of them during meditation we can give them a quick label, such as: "worrying" or "remembering" and dismiss them. Then they are gone.

Thoughts to which we attach sustained attention are held in place and fed. In meditation we can consciously choose to let these thoughts go and return to our repeated word. It is comforting to experience our power to ignore our judge's fearful thoughts. An ongoing practice of mediation creates a healthy discipline for being conscious and returning to center.

Meditation also allows us to notice the gaps between our thoughts. These quiet instants are non-verbal experiences of our conscious self. They are pleasant. Noticing them, we gently return our attention to our breath or repeated word.

Imagine behaving lovingly toward each thought, exactly as we would behave with a young child. Walking down the sidewalk holding the child's hand, we find that the child stops to look at things. We don't yank their arm. We gently remind them where we're going and begin to walk again.

After meditation we carry a heightened sense of awareness into the world. We realize that our unconscious mind is pumping thoughts, and that we can observe this process and make choices about it. From being caught in the flow, we have shifted to our non-judgmental observer, who is less reactive, less in the grip of our judge.

The practice of meditation is soothing to our judge. Since the poor guy works even while we're asleep, meditation is the only real rest he gets.

Alternatives

Some of us are visual, rather than auditory, learners. We can use creative visualization to focus attention on positive mental pictures. Imagination generates experience. Our judge believes an imagined picture as much as he believes sight. Our bodies react to our dreams, to the films we watch, and our mouths water when we vividly imagine food.

Shakti Gawain in her book, *Creative Visualization*, describes the key steps: set a goal, create a clear picture of it, focus on it often and give it positive energy. We can also put guided visualizations on audiotape. For those of us who prefer a kinesthetic way to communicate with our conscious selves, yoga and aikido are excellent.

Dialogging with Our Judge's Voices

We may find that we have two voices going back and forth in our heads. One voice is dissatisfied and wants to do something, but the other is afraid that change won't work. For example, Daniel regularly saw Tina in class and he was attracted to her:

Daniel voice #1: "I like Tina and would like to ask her to have coffee with me."

Daniel voice #2: "But I don't think she likes me. She'll say 'no' and I'll look like an idiot."

Daniel voice #1: "She looks friendly."

Daniel voice #2: "But she prefers to talk with Vince and Randy."

Let's look at another example. Julie was in business for herself. Here's how she got herself stuck when it came to letting people know about her business.

Julie voice #1: "I should market my services"

Julie voice #2: "I hate to sell, to brag. And what if they don't like my work anyway?"

Julie voice #1: "But I really offer a great service and do it well."

Julie voice #2: "I refuse to be a money-grubber."

Notice the nature of her self-talk. "I should" is a judgmental prod that can easily bring up resistance. "Brag" carries strong negative connotations. "What if they don't like my work" could easily set up a self-fulfilling prophecy. "Money-grubber" is a nasty put-down.

Unresolved inner conflicts such as these can go round and round, wearing us down, immobilizing us, even leading to depression. At such times we have a choice. We can become conscious and realize there is a feeling and hope behind each voice. Here is how Julie used conscious communication with her first voice.

Conscious self to voice #1: Are you upset because you were hoping to have more business, to have more money?"

Voice #1: "Yes, I want to do more of the work I love, but I'm afraid people won't like my work."

Conscious: "So you're fearful because you'd really like your work to be appreciated?"

Voice #1: "Yeah."

Julie's conscious self also spoke to Julie voice #2: "Are you uncomfortable with selling because you want to be perceived as modest and polite?"

Voice #2: "I don't want to be seen as brash, and I'm afraid if I build myself up to them, I won't meet their expectations."

Conscious: "So you're afraid of being judged negatively? You want to be honest and to have your customers feel satisfied?"

Voice #2: "Yes."

After this discussion with herself, Julie's thinking became clearer and less judgmental. Her two voices then saw ways to cooperate and Julie began to feel enthusiastic. She put together a flyer that accurately described her services and distributed it to people she considered likely to appreciate her work. When jobs came in, she scheduled her work to be certain she had enough time to do a thorough job for each customer.

When consciously communicating with ourselves, we don't jump in and try to solve our problem right away. Nor do we judge, attack or fight with a voice. We let each of our voices express their feelings and hopes. We hear them, and by doing so, our emotional blockage dissipates and our creative energy is free to move.

Meghan had been terrified of school and of public speaking. These fears had significantly handicapped her. With coaching she learned how to communicate with the voice in her head that was telling her, "You're going to make a fool of yourself." She discovered and satisfied the self-protective intention behind the voice. Not long after that she delivered a gripping speech to a college class. She was free of her old fears.

When we are upset, guilty, or afraid that we have made a mistake we are most in need of self-acceptance. Judges will be childlike; it is their nature. *To bring about change—love your judge.* Times to center yourself and talk silently to your judge include standing in the longest checkout lane at the supermarket and driving behind a slow car.

If we find we worry repeatedly and see no solution we can tell ourselves, "A solution is emerging," or "My hopes will continue to be met." Then we can turn our attention to something else and be receptive. When our heart is open to ourselves, it opens to others.

Conscious communication is a gift of love that affirms other people and ourselves. By initiating this positive cycle of affirmation, we have created a friendly universe.

Appendix

Summary

When do we use Conscious Communication?

Our first twinge that a conflict is brewing is the time to become conscious, because interpersonal conflict is a clear sign that our judge has made a negative judgment. We have two internal alarms:

- When we become aware of feeling fear, anger, or sadness in relation to another person.

- When we notice that we are being judgmental, holding a grievance or a vengeful thought.

When our judge is in gear, so is the other person's, making the situation potentially volatile.

What do we do?

We stop, center ourselves and focus on feelings and hopes, ours and the other person's. Then we listen, laugh, leave or speak, as our intuition tells us is appropriate.

We may talk to ourselves, listening to the voice of our judgmental thought and guessing at the feeling and hope behind it. We then discover that it was motivated by a positive hope for ourselves, the judge just stated the message harshly. We then reformulate the message to get our hope met.

Thinking this way redirects our mind to the remembrance of our essential goodness. As we do so we experience inner peace.

What we are not trying to do and why

We are not trying to use conscious communication to fix or change the other person. We are not trying to correct the other person. We are not trying to see their errors and forgive them. That would only separate us. To accuse someone else of attacking is to make a negative judgment and show that we entirely missed the point of what they are really asking for.

We realize that the apparent "attack" is our own misinterpretation; the problem is in our mind. Our interpretation is the only error that needs correction. We correct it by choosing to see the goodness in the other person, behind their words, and to accept them as they really are.

When we practice conscious communication it is best to deal with actual personal situations. Hypothetical examples are dangerous because they are fearful projections without a personal hope behind them.

We don't need to be conscious at every moment, nor do we need to use conscious communication all the time—we'd be exhausted. For example, if we are at the table and the food is bland, we don't say, "Mother, may I have your attention? I have an idea that I believe would enhance my appreciation of the meal. When I tried the potatoes I was disappointed because I was hoping for a stronger flavor. Would you be willing to pass me the salt?"

We just say "Please pass the salt."

When we have learned how to consciously override our judges, we are freed from rote application of the listening and speaking elements. Our manner becomes more fluid and we artfully use only those elements needed in a particular situation.

Why are relationships so important?

Because deep inside, we know that the quality of our relationships determines the quality of our lives. Our suspicion that this is so has been confirmed empirically by those who assess the quality of their lives most closely—people who know they are about to die. When surveyed about the things that matter most in life, ninety percent of the terminally ill put intimate relationships at the top of the list.

The joy of loving interchange experienced in healthy relationships might seem sufficient explanation for why this is so. But there is a more compelling reason: How other people see us determines our self image, whether we think of ourselves as a good person or bad.

Psychologists have documented that a positive self-image is the most important determiner of success and happiness in life. People with low self-esteem are unable to find supportive mates; they expect to be rejected, they don't pursue rewarding relationships, and they sabotage existing relationships. They also evaluate their own performance negatively and have difficulty defending themselves against negative comments.

From birth onward, it is the feedback we receive from others that tells us who we are. During millions of interpersonal interactions, whether we are consciously aware of it or not, we are about the business of influencing people to see us positively.

Must we stoop to being a "people pleaser"? No. People who attempt this lose their self-respect as well as the respect of others. There is a much more powerful and effective stance. Our satisfaction in life is entirely up to us, because how we communicate determines how other people see us, and how we view ourselves. Every interaction we have with someone either builds the relationship or harms it.

Although we all have the capacity to completely control our communication, few people do it well. To communicate effectively we need to understand the underlying psychology of interpersonal interactions and learn to use new skills. Without these we will continue to make mistakes, hurting others and ourselves.

Why does Conscious Communication seem to be difficult?

- Because we habitually listen to the judge's plan, which is to see the other person's wrong first and then attempt to correct or overlook it. We will see what we expect to see. In this way we choose our reality: attack or love.

- Because we habitually try to tell people what they are feeling or wanting. This is perceived by them as arrogance and precipitates defensive reactions. Instead we humbly and charitably guess at other people's positive truth.

- Because we fear that conscious communication is unnatural. When we first try it we feel awkward. The fear-based attack language of the judge is habitual, so we think it's natural. But with a little practice listening and speaking consciously, we become fluent. Conscious language is our means to share our feelings and hopes; it couldn't be more natural.

- Because the judge will scream, "You can't do this! Conscious communication won't work with this person, because he is so nasty he couldn't possibly respond positively to it." We learn to stop ourselves, breathe, and choose again.

What do we need in order to succeed?

Only willingness on our part is required. We need willingness to initiate conscious override, to guess at hopes, and to trust the process. Willingness is not required on the part of others, because now we know how to dispel the judge's cloudy layer of fear that is obscuring the light at their center.

Practice is the only way to learn a behavioral skill. Because we all make mistakes, awkwardness is to be expected at first. But as we practice we become more fluent in conscious communication. Here are some things to practice daily:

- Anytime you are having difficulty, listen to what you are saying to others and to yourself.

- Hear your judge's attacks.

- Replay the interaction in your mind, this time using conscious communication.

- Remember that it is never too late to connect at the level of feelings and hopes.

- Practice with your partner, family, friends, and strangers.

- Take a class in conscious communication.

- Form your own support group and meet periodically to practice and get feedback.

- Follow your own spiritual practice of meditation or prayer.

- Be kind.

What is the result?

- Resolved conflicts with solutions that work well for everyone

- Satisfying relationships based on genuine mutual appreciation

- Inner peace

Table 15 – Choices in Conscious Communication

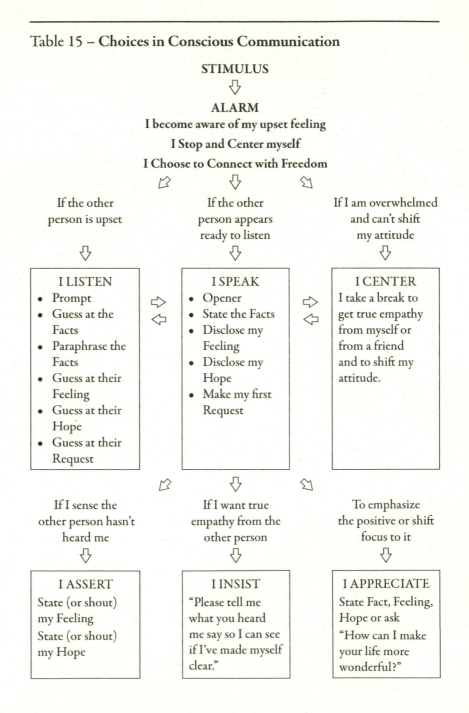

STIMULUS
⇩

ALARM
I become aware of my upset feeling
I Stop and Center myself
I Choose to Connect with Freedom

If the other
person is upset

If the other
person appears
ready to listen

If I am overwhelmed
and can't shift
my attitude

I LISTEN
- Prompt
- Guess at the Facts
- Paraphrase the Facts
- Guess at their Feeling
- Guess at their Hope
- Guess at their Request

I SPEAK
- Opener
- State the Facts
- Disclose my Feeling
- Disclose my Hope
- Make my first Request

I CENTER
I take a break to get true empathy from myself or from a friend and to shift my attitude.

If I sense the
other person hasn't
heard me

If I want true
empathy from the
other person

To emphasize
the positive or shift
focus to it

I ASSERT
State (or shout) my Feeling
State (or shout) my Hope

I INSIST
"Please tell me what you heard me say so I can see if I've made myself clear."

I APPRECIATE
State Fact, Feeling, Hope or ask "How can I make your life more wonderful?"

Practice Exercises

A Friend

Your friend tells you, "I stayed late to finish some work for my supervisor, but when I saw her the next day she didn't even mention it."

Now You Try It. What would say to your friend?

Some Judge Responses to A Friend

1. "How ungrateful."

2. "She may have just forgotten. You could drop a casual reminder."

3. "Well, we know how much you do for that company."

A Conscious Listening Response

"Are you disappointed because you were hoping for some appreciation?"

A Co-worker

You take a new job and are really working hard to get up to speed. Your co-worker, Betsy, gradually begins turning more and more tasks over to you. One day she asks you to do some filing and the next morning you learn that that filing is really her job.

Now You Try It. What you would say to Betsy?

Some Judge Responses to A Friend

1. Just ignore it, hoping something like that won't happen again.

2. "Hey Betsy, that filing isn't my job."

3. "I resent being taken advantage of."

A Conscious Listening Response

You: "Betsy, I have an idea I think would help with the work flow. Do you have a minute?"

Betsy: "OK."

You: "I didn't mind doing that filing yesterday, but today I felt a little confused when I learned that it was part of your job."

Betsy: "Oh yeah, I had some high-priority work to do and thought you'd be able to get it done. That way we can get everything done in the department."

You: "I see. Well, I like the idea that we can fill in for each other. Next time I'd prefer it if you asked me. Then I could feel good about lending you a hand. How does that sound to you?"

A Child

Your ten-year-old son is playing a game and you have told him you both have to leave at 3:45 for his dental appointment. The time rolls around and you tell him it's time to go.

He cries out: "No! I have to finish this."

Now You Try It. What you would say to your son?

Some Judge Responses to A Child

1. "I told you that you had to be ready at 3:45. Look, it's 3:45. Now let's go!"

2. "You can finish that when we get back."

3. "You come right now or no TV tonight."

A Conscious Response

You: "Are you upset because you really want to finish what you're doing?"

Son: "Yes!"

You: "Gee, I wish you had the time to do it now. (pause) If we don't get to the dentist on time we'll miss your appointment and then I would be embarrassed and very upset. We have to go right now to make it. I'll make sure you have time to finish your game when we get home. Here, I'll help you put your coat on."

A Depressed Person

George, your friend and racquetball partner, has stopped calling you. He was divorced and then he told you that he had been laid off. He canceled out of the last racquetball game and you've been meaning to call him.

You meet George on the street and say, "Hi George. It's good to see you. How are you?"

"I've been better."

"Let's get a cup of coffee."

"OK."

As you sit down with the coffee, you say, "So tell me how things are going."

George briefly catches your eye and then looks down at his cup. "I've never felt worse in my whole life," he replies. "I feel like giving up."

Now You Try It. What you would say to George?

Some Judge Responses to A Depressed Person

1. "Oh George, don't give up."

2. Naturally you're upset, with all that's happened to you. But none of it is your fault. Let's play racquetball tomorrow. What do you say?"

3. "Hey, it's not that bad, George. I know a great ... (job placement service, available woman, therapist, etc.)

A Conscious Listening Response

"You feel so bad you want to quit?"   Paraphrase

"Nothing works," George replies, "I've destroyed my family and now I'm too depressed to look for work."

"How awful. Are you sad because you want the loving support you had in your family?"   Guess at hope

"No, my wife wasn't supportive."

"So tell me what's going on."   Prompt

"I feel terrible about what happened to the kids. It's been hardest on them."

"How are they?"

"That's the worst part. I only get to see them once a week. I know they're hurting, but they don't want to talk about it."

"So you feel bad when you see them that way. You'd like to be able to make them happy?"   Guess at hope

"More than anything in this world."

An Unresponsive Mate

In general, your husband, Jason, has shown a disappointing lack of intimacy. You wish that he would talk with you at a feeling level.

You just came home, very excited, from seeing a film, in which a teacher's love for a handicapped girl inspired the girl to achieve and lead a wonderful life. You find Jason in the kitchen getting a snack.

As you enthusiastically start telling him about the film you notice he doesn't seem to be very interested. So you describe it in richer detail to make it more vivid for him. Jason stands up, says, "I'd like to eat this in the other room," and begins to turn away.

You say, "Jason, hey wait a minute. I want to share this story with you. Don't you want to hear it?"

He sighs and says, "Can you make it quick?"

Now You Try It. What would you say to Jason.

Some Judge Responses

1. "OK, I'll sum it up. But then I can't convey the real meaning of it."

2. "When you don't listen to me when I have something important to say, I feel really irritated."

3. "Why aren't you interested in things that I find truly moving and beautiful?"

A Conscious Listening Response:

"Would you rather have private time to eat?"	Guess at hope
"I don't mind if you come join me," replies Jason.	
You both sit down in the other room.	
"Jason, when I was telling you about the film were you feeling a little uncomfortable?"	Guess at feeling
"A little, yeah."	
"I'd like to know how you were feeling so we can communicate better next time. "Would you be willing to tell me what it was that you felt uncomfortable about?"	Prompt for fact
"You get so dramatic about it. Why can't you just tell me what it was about?"	
"So when I get dramatic, really enthusiastic, you feel uncomfortable?"	Paraphrase fact and feeling
"Yeah. It's not so much you being enthusiastic, but look, I wasn't there. It's not my kind of thing. I can't get as excited about it as you'd like me to be."	

"Are you uncomfortable because you think
I want a response from you that would be
different from how you really feel?"

Guess at his hope
(to be authentic)

"Yeah. I'm just not that excited about it."

"Would you like me to simply relate what
I did in a briefer, more matter of fact
way?"

Guess at his request

"Yeah."

"Would you be willing to hear how I feel
when I hear that from you?"

Request

"OK."

"I feel sad because I want to be able to
share things at a feeling level that mean a
lot to me. How do you feel in response to
that?"

Feeling
Hope
Request

"Like here comes the old lecture about
how I'm not good enough. How you want
someone you can get all emotional with
about stuff I haven't seen and can't relate
to. Well I'm sorry. That's just not me."

"So are you hoping that I'll let you be who
you are and not expect you to change?"

Guess at hope

"I think you want me to be this real
sensitive guy who gets all exited, jumps up
and down, and cries on a dime whenever
you want him to."

"Oh, I just want to be able to share things
at a feeling level."

Hope
Guess at feeling

"Are you afraid if we start looking at our
feelings that I won't like you? That I won't
find you to be good enough?"

"Yeah."

Endnotes

Page 5. Viktor E. Frankl, *Man's Search for Meaning,* New York: Simon and Schuster, Inc. 1984, pp. 86-87.

Page 6. Psychology training program. A program at Associates for Human Resources in Concord, MA under the auspices of Beacon College, accredited with the Commission of Higher Education, Middle States Association of Colleges and Schools, 1982. This program is no longer available.

Page 22. Freudian Psychology. This summary is adapted from Calvin S. Hall, *A Primer of Freudian Psychology*, New York: Mentor, 1979.

Page 29. Bargh, John A. lead article in *The Automaticity Of Everyday Life, Advances in Social Cognition*, Volume X, Robert S. Wyer, Jr., editor, Mahwah, New Jersey: Erlbaum, 1997. P. 23. Bargh's work verified and expanded on research first performed by Dr. Russell Fazio, a psychologist at Indiana University in Bloomington.

Fazio, R. H. "How do Attitudes Guide Behavior?" In R. M. Sorrentino & E. T. Higgins (Eds.) *Handbook of Motivation and Cognition* (Vol. 1, pp. 204-243), New York: Guilford, 1986.

The list of liked and disliked words was developed by Dr. Mahzarin Banaji at Yale University.

Page 30. Unconscious processing faster. Neely, J. H. "Semantic Priming and Retrieval from Lexical Memory," *Journal of Experimental Psychology: General*, 106, 226-254, 1977.

Page 31 Everything one encounters. Bargh, *Automaticity*, op. cit. P. 23.

Page 32. What our unconscious does. Bargh, John A. *Automaticity*. pp. 6-35.

Page 33. Judgment determines feeling. Niedenthal, Paula M. "Affect and Social Perception: On the Psychological Validity of Rose-Colored Glasses," in Bornstein & Pttman, Eds., *Perception Without Awareness*, New York: Guilford, 1992.

Goal setting. Bargh, *Automaticity*, p. 39-45

Page 34. Sexual aggression and power. Bargh, *Automaticity*, p. 46-47

Page 35. Goals operate unconsciously. Bargh, *Automaticity*, p. 41.

Goals direct social behavior. Bargh, *Automaticity*, p. 47.

Judgements counter to intent. Bargh, *Automaticity*, p. 43.

Influenced to be rude. Bargh, J. A., Chen, M., & Burrows, L., "Automaticity of Social Behavior", *Journal of Personality and Social Psychology*, 71, 230-244, 1996.

Approach and withdrawal. Bargh, J. A., Chen, M., & Burrows, L., "Automaticity of Social Behavior", *Journal of Personality and Social Psychology*, 71, 230-244, 1996.

Hypnotized woman. E. R. Hilgard, *Divided Consciousness*, New York: Wiley, 1977.

Page 36. Ninety-nine percent. Bargh, *Automaticity*, p. 2 and 244.

Page 37. Overestimating deliberate control. Bargh, *Automaticity*, p. 244.

Page 42. Unconscious contains patterns. C. G. Jung, *Basic Postulates of Analytical Psychology*, 1931, p. 349.

Historical prejudice. C. G. Jung, *The Structure of the Psyche*, 1928, p. 157.

Prejudice. *The American Heritage Dictionary of the English Language,* Third Edition, 1992.

Page 43. Shared beliefs. Erving Goffman suggested another way to look at it. We view everything through our "interpretive frameworks." We give meaning to our experience as we structure the experience into a story. We use language to do this and our language has a stock of culturally available interpretations that are considered appropriate and relevant. Erving Goffman, *Frame Analysis,* New York: Harper, 1974. We use a language of separation and fault-finding, of judgment and blame. It is a language that sees "wrongs" carried out by people with bad intentions who need to be resisted, punished, and/or corrected.

Culture directs perception. Bargh, *Automaticity*, p. 244.

Experiment with students. Dov Cohen, in Wyer, *Automaticity*, p. 123.

Chronic framework. Bargh, in Higgins, E. Tory and Kruglanski, Arie, *Social Psychology: Handbook of Basic Principles*, New York: Guilford, 1996. P. 178.

Page 44. Man in forest. Professor Dov Cohen references this study by Turnbull on page 122 of Wyer, *Automaticity*.

Page 46. Greatest pupil dilation. E. H. Hess and J. M. Polt, "Pupil size as related to Interest Value of Visual Stimuli," *Science 132*, 1960, 349-350.

Liking dilated pupils. Niedenthal, P. M. & Cantor, N. "Affective Responses as Guides to category-based influences," *Motivation and Emotion*, 10, 217-259.

Detecting emotional expression unconsciously. Bargh, John A. lead article in *The Automaticity Of Everyday Life, Advances in Social Cognition*, Volume X, Robert S. Wyer, Jr., editor, Mahwah, New Jersey: Erlbaum, 1997. p. 20.

Page 48. Meanings not present in objective world. Ibid. p. 9.

Explaining to lay friend. Ibid. p. 243.

Page 52. Tragedy. *The American Heritage Dictionary of the English Language, Third Edition*, Boston: Houghton Mifflin Company, 1992

Page 59. Conscious override. Bargh states "The only factor which affect[s] unconscious judgment [is] conscious processing, i.e. choosing to consciously think about the judgment rather than unconsciously react." *Automaticity*, op. cit. p. 25. We currently do this only about one percent of the time. We can learn to do it more frequently.

Page 60-61. "I have a body..." Susan S. Trout, Ph.D., *To See Differently: Personal Growth and Being of Service Through Attitudinal Healing*, Washington, D.C.: Three Roses Press, 1990, pp. 95-96. Adapted from an exercise of Roberto Assagioli, *The Act of Will*, New York: Viking, 1974, pp. 214-216.

"We need not identify with each thought. Ram Dass and Paul Gorman, *How Can I Help?* New York: Knopf, 1985, p. 99.

"We dis-identify by observing..." Piero Ferrucci, *What We May Be*, Los Angeles: Tarcher, 1982, p. 65.

Page 62. With sense of wholeness we enhance relationship. Abraham H. Maslow, *Toward a Psychology of Being*, Second Edition, New York: Van Nostrand Reinhold, 1969. Maslow studied people who were psychologically very healthy and made two basic discoveries: that our inner nature is neutral or "good" and that we have a natural drive toward optimal psychological health. He also found that people had two different levels of needs.

Deficit needs occur when a specific goal (food, safety) is seen outside the body. In this case scarcity is assumed and fear is the motivator. Interpersonally this results in attempting to "get" something from someone or manipulate them. There is a concurrent tendency to categorize or judge.

Growth needs are abstract (wholeness, playfulness) and the goal is determined in the mind. Abundance is assumed and joy is the motivator. Interpersonally this results in helping other people with a concurrent tendency to see them more objectively and to accept them as they are. Growth motivation characterizes "self-actualizing" people and occurs about one percent of the time.

Page 62-63. "It has been my experience that persons have a basically positive direction... " Carl Rogers, *On Becoming A Person*, pp. 37-38.

Page 65. Income up but happiness down. David G. Myers, Scripps Howard News Service, January 17, 1998.

We all want to be recognized. Maslow, loc. cit. P. 93.

Page 68. Baumeister, *Losing Control*, pages 27 and 244.

Page 74. Re: Carl Rogers. According to Howard Kirschenbaum, author of *On Becoming Carl Rogers*, New York: Delacorte, 1979, Rogers gave credit to his wife, Helen, for providing him with the empathic support that enabled him to fulfill his illustrious career.

Pages 76-77. Listening situation. Adapted form Faber & Mazlish, *How to Talk so Kids Will Listen*.

Page 80. This model has similarities with Daniel Goleman's Emotional Competence Framework, *Working with Emotional Intelligence*, New York: Bantam, 1998, p. 26-27.

Page 90. Understanding a person. Thich Nhat Hahn, *Living Buddha, Living Christ*, New York: Riverhead books, 1995, p. 85.

"Love is really listening." Jampolsky, Gerald G., MD, "Surrendering to Love," *Daily Word*, Vol. 135, No. 4, p.10, Unity Village, MO: Unity School of Christianity, 1997.

Page 92-93. Ram Dass and Paul Gorman, *How Can I Help? Stories and Reflections on Service*, New York: Alfred A. Knopf, 1993, P. 66-67, 68.

Page 95. Model for helpful listening. Robert R. Carkhuff, *The Art of Helping*, Seventh Edition, Amherst, MA: Human Development Press, Inc. 1993, 109-148.

Page 99. I-message example. Dr. Thomas Gordon, P. E. T. *Parent Effectiveness Training*, New York: Peter H. Wyden, Inc., 1970. p. 136.

The concept originated with Hiam Ginott, *Between Parent and Child*, New York: Avon Books, 1965.

Page 107. The verb "to be." Adapted from Albert Ellis, Ph.D., *Anger: How to Live With and Without It*, 1977.

Page 109. Anger "highjack," Daniel Goleman, *Emotional Intelligence*, 1995, p. 13.

Page 112. "When you forgot to pick up my clothes..." Goleman states this "is an expression of basic emotional intelligence..." Emotional Intelligence, 1995, Daniel Goleman, p.135.

Page 115. Emotional slavery, an aspect of codependence, is a condition in which we think we cause other people's feelings and look to find the truth about ourselves in other peoples' judges. See *Facing Codependence* by Pia Mellody with Andrea Wells Miller and J. Keith Miller.

Page 120. In the French language, from which our word "please" is derived, the whole phrase, *s'il vous plait*, is still used.

Page 122. To help other people get their hopes met. "At times helping [others is] simply.. not something we really think about, merely the instinctive response of an open heart. Caring is a reflex... Expressing our innate generosity, we experience our "kin"-ship, our "kind"-ness. It was "Us." In service, we taste unity... Caring for one another, we sometimes glimpse an essential quality of our being... We're reminded of who we really are and what we have to offer one another." Ram Dass and Paul Gorman, *How Can I Help? Stories and Reflections on Service*, New York: Knopf, 1993.

For more on generosity see *Wherever You Go There You Are*, by Jon Kabat-Zinn, p. 61-64.

Page 128. Rather be killed than branded a wimp. "Because shame is such an undesirable experience, I have found that boys (and men) will do anything to avoid the possibility of experiencing it.." William Pollack, *Real Boys: Rescuing Our Sons for the Myths of Boyhood*, New York: Random House, 1998.

Eighty percent emotionally numb. Ron Levant, psychologist, attribution by Terrence Real in *I Don't Want to Talk About It: Overcoming the Legacy of Male Depression*, New York: Scribner, 1997. See R. Levant and G. Kopecky, Masculinity Reconstructed, New York: Penguin, 1995.

See also Daniel Goleman, Emotional Intelligence, page 50

Male acculturation. For a fascinating historical account of male socialization see Riane Eisler, *The Chalice and the Blade*, San Francisco: HarperSanFrancisco, 1987.

Page 129. Incompetence in relationships. Milder stereotypical male communication patterns are described by Deborah Tannen,, *You Just Don't Understand: Men and Women in Conversation*, New York: Ballantine Books, 1990.

Page 131. Empathy. *The American Heritage Dictionary*.

Page 132. Drunk story. Adapted from Terry Dobson with Judith Shepherd-Chow, *Safe and Alive*, Los Angeles: J. P. Tarcher, Inc., 1981. Pages 128-132.

Page 134. Anger. Daniel Goleman, in his book *Emotional Intelligence,* describes the physiological process by which anger can "hijack" our minds.

Page 135. Power definition. Bargh, *Automaticity*, p. 45.

Page 138. Marshall B. Rosenberg, *Facilitator's Manual for Nonviolent Communication, Basic Skills Program*, 1992.

Page 150. The Golden Rule in World Religions. Compiled by Dorothy Grant.

Page 153. Body is unconscious mind. Candace B. Pert, Ph.D., *Molecules of Emotion: Why You Feel the Way You Do*, New York: Scribner, 1997. P. 141, 146, 147.

"Spirit" "Incorporeal" *The American Heritage Dictionary*.

Page 154-6. Mexican bandit story. This is my recollection of the story Robert told. Robert Gass subsequently published the story, "Guests in the Night," in *A 3rd Serving of Chicken Soup for the Soul*, Jack Canfield and Mark Hansen, Eds., Deerfield Beach, FL: Health Communications, Inc., 1996.

Page 157. Love. *The American Heritage Dictionary*.

Page 159. Moving articles. Michaud, Stephen G., "To Bait a Killer," *Reader's Digest*, June, 1995; Jerome, Richard, with Anne Maier, Bob Stewart and Vickie Bane, "No Reprieve," People, August 26, 1996.

Page 159-60. Becker, Kathy, "The Gift of Forgiveness," *Miracles*, Number Six, October, 1993.

Desmond Tutu. Quoted in articles by Kurt Shillinger in *The Christian Science Monitor* on July 3, 1998.

Page 161. Reflective Forgiveness Exercise. Adapted from *A Course in Miracles*, Workbook lesson 134.

Visual Forgiveness Exercise. Adapted from *A Course in Miracles*, Workbook lesson 121.

Choose to see the love. In Lee Harper's novel, *To Kill a Mockingbird*, the loving and wise father, Atticus, tells his daughter she can never know anybody until she has "walked around in his skin" for a while. She learned the lesson.

Page 163. Dr. John Cacioppo. *New York Times*, December 15, 1992.

Page 166. Expectations of partner. "You automatically trigger feelings of unhappiness when the people and situations around you do not fit your expectations. In other words, expectations create your unhappiness. It's the emotion backed demands that make you suffer—it's not the world, the people around you or even you yourself." Ken Keyes, Jr. and Bruce Burkan, *How to Make Your Life Work Or Why Aren't You Happy?* Coos Bay , OR: Living Love Publications, 1974.

Page 171. Men can nurture. Kyle D. Pruett, M. D., *The Nurturing Father*, New York: Warner, 1987.

There are no differences. William Pollack, Real Boys: *Rescuing Our Sons from the Myths of Boyhood*, New York: Random House, 1998, P. 116.

Gender-stereotyped assumptions about communication are not helpful. In 1997, scholars Daniel Canary and Tara Emmers-Sommer reviewed the existing research on sex and gender stereotypes for their book *Sex and Gender Differences* in Personal Relationships, New York: Guilford, 1997. While all of the research is subjective, they state that no sex differences can be predicted unless all of the following hold: sex relevant beliefs are activated, they are consistent with sex stereotypes, there are no competing moderators and no alternative relational expectations, and the partner's prior behavior did not promote a sex-stereotypic response. They concluded: "stereotypes present an outdated view of men and women that distorts scientific understandings of male and female interactions, especially in the context of personal relationships."

Page 172. Charitable intentions. J.C. Pearson, "Positive Distortion: The Most Beautiful Woman in the World," in *Making Connections: Readings in Interpersonal Communication*, K. M. Gavin and P. Cooper, eds. Beverly Hills, CA: Roxbury, 1996, pp. 175-181. In her book, *Lasting Love: What Keeps Couples Together*, Pearson writes, "If people could only learn one lesson about lasting love, they would probably be best served by learning about unconditional acceptance... Couples who positively distort their partner's communication behavior are more satisfied with their marriage than couples who do not distort their partner's behavior." (Pages 54, 73) By "distort," Pearson means choose to find a positive motivation when one is not readily apparent.

Page 173-5. Jo Ann Larsen. This story appeared in *Chicken Soup for the Soul*, edited by Jack Canfield and Mark Victor Hansen, Deerfield Beach, FL: Health Communications, Inc., 1993

Page 180. Love is "The will to extend one's self for the purpose of nurturing one's own or another's spiritual growth." When we do this relationships can become the vehicle for our emotional and spiritual healing. M. Scott Peck, *The Road Less Traveled: A New Psychology of Love*, Traditional Values and Spiritual Growth, New York: Touchstone, 1978.

Love allows us to see the very essence of another human being. We can see their potential and help them to actualize Viktor Frankl, *Man's Search for Meaning*, p. 176-177

Page 185-6. Teach connection. William Pollack, *Real Boys: Rescuing Our Sons from the Myths of Boyhood*, New York: Random House, 1998, P. xxiv.

Recommendations adapted from Pollack, pages 47-51.

Page 187. Principles of Aikido. Morihei Ueshiba, the founder of aikido said, about harmonious use of energy, "Nothing less than becoming one with the universe will suffice."

Attacks as energy gifts. Thomas F. Crum, *The Magic of Conflict*, New York: Simon and Schuster, 1987, p.41

Page 192. "Work Reflections" from an interview with Dick Leader, *Fast Company* Magazine Feb/Mar, 1998

Page 197. Fifteen year study. Ferdinand F. Fournies, *Why Employees Don't Do What They're Supposed to Do And What to Do About It*. Blue Ridge Summit, PA: Liberty House, 1988.

Page 201. Let Davidson, Wisdom At Work: The Awakening of Consciousness in the Workplace, Burdett, NY: Larson Publications, 1998. P. 19. See also D. A. Infante, B. L. Riddle, C. L. Horvath, and S. A. Tumlin, "Verbal Aggressiveness: Messages and Reasons," *Communication Quarterly*, 40 (1992): 116-126. Learning how to constructively resolve disagreements at work has also been shown to enhance self-concept: A. S. Rancer, R. L. Kosberg, and R. A. Baukus, "Beliefs About Arguing As Predictors of Trait Argumentativeness: Implications for Training in Argument and Conflict Management," *Communication Education* 41 (1992): 375-387.

"Triple-crown." Bridget O'Brian, "Southwest Airlines Is a Rare Carrier: It Still Makes Money," The Wall Street Journal, October 26, 1992. This reference and the next are taken from Jeffrey Pfeffer, *Competitive Advantage through People: Unleashing the Power of the Workforce*, Boston: Harvard Business School Press, 1994.

Top stock return. "Investment Winners and Losers," *Money*, October 1992, 133.

X-ray vision. Let Davidson, *Wisdom At Work: The Awakening of Consciousness in the Workplace*, Burdett, NY: Larson Publications, 1998. P. 89

Page 205. Love heals. Bernie Siegel, *Love, Medicine and Miracles*, New York: Harper & Row, 1986.

Page 206. Confirming self-image. B. Bower, "Truth Aches: People Who View Themselves Poorly May Seek the Truth and Find Despair," *Science News*, August 15, 1992: 110-111; and W. B. Swann, R. M. Wenzlaff, D. S. Krull, and B. W. Pelham, "Allure of Negative Feedback: Self-Verification Strivings Among Depressed Persons." *Journal of Abnormal Psychology* 101, 1992: p. 293-306.

Seek out people who confirm. In *The Psychology of Romantic Love*, Nathaniel Branden writes, "If we do not love ourselves, it is almost impossible to believe fully that we are loved by someone else... No matter what our partner does to show that he or she cares, we do not experience the devotion as convincing because we do not feel lovable to ourselves."

Page 297. Research proves people sabotage. J. Kolligan, Jr., "Perceived Fraudulence as a Dimension of Perceived Incompetence," in *Competence Considered*, R. J. Sternberg and J. Kolligan, Jr., eds., New Haven: Yale University Press, 1990.

See self as rejected. G. Downey and S. J. Feldman, "Implications of Rejection Sensitivity for Intimate Relationships," *Journal of Personality and Social Psychology* 70, 1996, p. 1327-1343.

Page 210. Self-Talk. Shad Helmstetter, *What to Say When You Talk to Yourself*, Scottsdale, AZ: Grindle Press, 1986.

Page 211-12. Some books on meditation: Jon Kabat-Zinn, *Wherever You Go, There You Are: Mindfulness Meditation*, New York: Hyperion, 1994. Ram Dass, *Journey of Awakening: A Meditator's Guidebook*, revised edition, New York: Bantam Books, 1990. Joseph Goldstein, *The Experience of Insight: A Natural Unfolding*, Santa Cruz: Unity Press, 1976. Jack Kornfield, A Path With Heart, New York: Bantam, 1993. Lawrence LeShan, *How to Meditate: A Guide to Self-Discovery*, New York: Bantam Books, 1975.

Shakti Gawain, *Creative Visualization*, New York: Bantam, 1982.

Page 219. Study of terminally ill. C. Edward Crowther and G. Stone, *Intimacy: Strategies for Successful Relationships*, Santa Barbara, CA: Capra Press, 1986. P. 13.

People with low self-esteem. B. Bower, "Truth Aches: People Who View Themselves Poorly May Seek the 'Truth' and Find Despair," Science News, August 15, 1992, p. 110-111.

See also J. Kolligan, Jr., "Perceived Fraudulence as a Dimension of Perceived Incompetence," in Competence Considered, R. J. Sternberg and J. Kolligan, Jr., eds., New Haven, CT: Yale University Press, 1990.

Immune system. "A lack of diverse social contacts is a stronger risk factor for colds than smoking, low vitamin C intake, or elevated stress hormones... Research suggests that people with or without the stress of illness enjoy better health and a better quality of life when they get emotional support through a network of friends, relatives, and associates or through structured groups." *Harvard Health Letter*, Boston: Harvard Medical School Health Publications Group, April, 1998. P. 1,3.

Life itself. In order to find out if there was an original language, Fredrick II conducted an experiment with a group of babies. He had foster mothers breast feed them and wash them but not talk to them. Lacking interpersonal communication, all the children died. J. B. Ross and M. M. McLaughlin, eds. *A Portable Medieval Reader*, New York: Viking, 1949.

Also, prisoners of war deprived of communication die sooner, E. B. McDaniel with J. Johnson, *Scars and Stripes*, Philadelphia: A. J. Holman, 1975, p. 40.

Bibliography

Bargh, John A., "The Automaticity of Everyday Life" in Wyer, Robert S., (Ed.) *The Automaticity of Everyday Life, Advances in Social Cognition*, Volume X, Mahwah, NJ: Erlbaum, 1997.

Benson, Herbert, *Timeless Healing: The Power and Biology of Belief*, New York: Fireside, 1996.

Berke, Diane, *Love Always Answers: Walking the Path of "Miracles,"* New York: Crossroad, 1994.

Briggs, Dorothy C., *Your Child's Self-Esteem,* New York: Doubleday, 1970.

Casarjian, Robin, *Forgiveness: A Bold Choice for a Peaceful Heart*, New York: Bantam Books, 1992.

Casarjian, Robin, *Houses of Healing: A Prisoner's Guide to Inner Power and Freedom*, Boston, MA: The Lionheart Foundation, 1995

Chappell, Tom, *The Soul of a Business: Managing for Profit and the Common Good*, New York: Bantam, 1993.

Crum, Thomas F., *The Magic of Conflict*, New York: Simon and Schuster, 1987.

A Course in Miracles, Second Edition, Foundation for Inner Peace, New York: Viking Penguin, 1996.

Davidson, Let, *Wisdom at Work: the Awakening of Consciousness in the Workplace*, Burdett, NT: Larson Publications, 1998.

Frankl, Viktor E., *Man's Search for Meaning*, New York: Simon and Schuster, Inc. 1984

Goldsmith, Joel S., *The Infinite Way*, Marina del Rey, California: DeVorss Publications, 1947.

Goleman, Daniel, *Emotional Intelligence*, New York: Bantam Books, 1995.

Goleman, Daniel, *Emotional Intelligence at Work*, New York, Bantam Books, 1998.

Gordon, Thomas, *P.E.T.: Parent Effectiveness Training*, New York: Peter Wyden, Inc., 1970.

Jampolsky, Gerald, *Change Your Mind, Change Your Life: Concepts in Attitudinal Healing*, New York: Bantam, 1993.

Jampolsky, Gerald, *Love Is Letting Go of Fear*, Millbrae, CA: Celestial Arts, 1979.

Jampolsky, Gerald, *Love Is the Answer: Creating Positive Relationships*, New York: Bantam Books, Inc. 1990.

Pollack, William, *Real Boys: Rescuing Our Sons from the Myths of Boyhood*, New York: Random House, 1998.

Powell, John, *The Secret of Staying in Love: Loving Relationships through Communication*, Allen, TX: Tabor Publishing, 1974.

Real, Terrence, *I Don't Want to Talk About It: Overcoming the Legacy of Male Depression*, New York: Scribner, 1997.

Remen, Rachel Naomi, *Kitchen Table Wisdom: Stories that Heal*, New York: Riverhead Books, 1996.

Rosenberg, Marshall, B. *Nonviolent Communication: A Language of Compassion*, Del Mar, CA: PuddleDancer Press, 1999.

Rogers, Carl R., *On Becoming a Person*, Boston: Houghton Mifflin, 1961.

Satir, Virginia, *Making Contact*, Millbrae, CA: Celestial Arts, 1976.

Spence, Jerry, *How to Argue and Win Every Time*, New York, St. Martin's Press, 1995.

Trout, Susan, *To See Differently: Personal Growth and Being of Service through Attitudinal Healing*, Washington, DC: Three Roses Press, 1990. Institute for Attitudinal Studies.

Index